Advance Praise for *JOURNEYING* . . .

"This is an important book. It brings to modern psychology the wisdom of the shaman, which has been 50,000 years in the making. It provides a landmark application of this wisdom to early developmental wounding where the ills of society begin. Anyone interested in the future of psychology should read this book."

Larry Dossey, MD
Author of *Prayer Is Good Medicine* and *Recovering the Soul*

"Shamans in indigenous cultures were and are also the psychologists of the community. In our culture we have split the roles. It's time to marry the systems together, and Jeannette Gagan through her expertise shows us how. *Journeying* is beautifully written."

Sandra Ingerman, MA
Author of *Soul Retrieval: Mending the Fragmented Self* and *A Fall to Grace*

"In these times of spiritual awakening, this book serves as a beacon lighting the path, unifying into one complete circle the cycles of pain into the realities of healing body, mind and spirit."

Grandmother Waynonah Two Worlds
Native American elder of the Bear Clan Lodge

"Impressive in its scope and depth, this text provides a new way of looking at the origins of psychotherapy and an understanding of shamanic healing in terms that are relevant to contemporary culture and psychology."

Larry G. Peters, PhD
Psychologist, ethnologist, and professor

"In this phenomenal book Jeannette Gagan gives us a psychological picture of the power of shamanic healing. Specifically, she shows how the separating and controlling energy of violence transforms into healing unity. This is 'must reading' as we work toward a world of illumination and cooperation for the coming millennium."

Twylah Nitsch
Seneca elder and granddaughter of Moses and Alice Shongo

JOURNEYING

JOURNEYING

Where Shamanism and Psychology Meet

Jeannette M. Gagan, PhD

RIO CHAMA PUBLICATIONS

Santa Fe, NM

Published by: **Rio Chama Publications**
PO Box 4276
Santa Fe, NM 87502

Editor: Ellen Kleiner
Book design and typography: Richard Harris
Cover art and chapter headings: Joe Gagan
Cover production: Janice St. Marie

A Blessingway book

The subject matter of this book does not constitute a substitute for psychotherapy.

Printed in the United States of America on acid-free recycled paper

Publisher's Cataloging-in-Publication Data
Gagan, Jeannette M.
    Journeying : where shamanism and psychology meet / by
    Jeannette M. Gagan.
        p. cm.
        Includes bibliographical references and index.
        Preassigned LCCN: 97-92496
        ISBN: 0-9642088-0-6

    1. Psychology, Applied.   2. Shamanism.   3. Spirituality.   4.
    Psychotherapy.   I. Title.

        BF1611.G34 1998   158.1
                                                  QB197-2025

10 9 8 7 6 5 4 3 2 1

This book is lovingly dedicated to my children,
their partners in life, and my grandchildren.

I am indebted to many people for their help in bringing this book to fruition. First and foremost, my editor Ellen Kleiner, who midwifed my journey from cloistered writer to public author with great inspiration and expertise; my friend and colleague Marythelma Brainard, whose enduring support and academic insight enriched this manuscript; my mentor and longtime sister of the desert, hills, and arroyos, Lesley Poling-Kempes; my neighbors and friends Al and Kathie Lostetter, whose example and encouragement sustained me through creative impasses. A special word of thanks to my Tuesday noon consultation group for their ongoing interest and feedback; to Deanne Kreis-Newman for her gracious guidance; to Kathleen Hart for her belief in my work; to Anne Scholder for her suggestions and support; to Sandra Ingerman for her shamanic mentoring and integrity; and to Grandmother Twylah for her teachings.

This project has further benefited from the assistance and input of Clifford Morgan, John Poling, Hugh Mithra Grubb, Linda Leaman, Ellen Lefkowitz, V. J. Montanye, R. J. Gagan, Rafe Martin, Kitty Farmer, Jill Hoelting, Carol MacHendrie, and Richard Harris.

Ultimately, without my clients, this book would not have come into being. With deep gratitude I honor their work, their growth, and all they have taught me. For those who so willingly allowed their dilemmas and journeys to be shared in an anonymous fashion, may blessings be returned tenfold.

Contents

Introduction

THIS IS NEITHER A SELF-HELP NOR A HOW-TO BOOK. RATHER, IT DESCRIBES areas of intersection between two healing arenas generally thought to be divergent while actually sharing certain features. These commonalities not only help define what we may think of as out-of-the-ordinary experiences but also spark theoretical interest in the dynamics underlying shamanic and psychological endeavors.

Whether you are a novice interested in healing pursuits, a veteran healer, or an individual invested in the exchange of information across healing modalities, you are likely to relate in one way or another to this viable perspective. Besieged, as you no doubt are, by hundreds of healing modalities, the illumination of a linkage between present-day psychology and the oldest healing tradition known to man will help you hold firmly to the relevance of nontraditional healing methods and of preventive approaches to mental health.

If you are versed in shamanism, you will tread familiar terrain in these chapters, although you will also come upon psychologically expanded interpretations of certain shamanic endeavors that

1

may blur the conventional boundaries set between shamanism and psychology. Psychologists, too, will recognize much of this turf. If you are empirically oriented, you may be disturbed by the speculative leap into domains difficult, if not impossible, to quantify. If, on the other hand, you are among those who yearn for a more spiritually inclusive psychology, you may discover new paths of least resistance. If you are a psychotherapist* in the "healing trenches," you are apt to resonate with much of this material as the healing phenomenon, no matter how it is defined, speaks its own symbolic language.

Writing this book was akin to reining in a wild horse accustomed to freely roaming a variety of landscapes. Chapter 1 presents the nature and history of shamanism and psychology. Chapter 2 describes shared methodologies and healing tenets. Readers who are not particularly interested in delving into the history and politics of psychology, specific healing approaches, altered states of consciousness, imagery, and the role of the unconscious may want to skip and scan through these pages.

Chapters 3 and 4 take a turn into the canyons and precipices of infant and early childhood experiences and their effects on adult behavior. Herein lies the heart of the book—the beating of the hooves against the earth—where shamanic healing is applied to developmental wounding. In chapter 3 this wounding, which results from inadequate bonding with parental figures, including outright neglect or abuse, is shown as a root cause of dysfunction and of the flagrant displays of aggression that so diminish our society. Case examples portray how shamanic journeying actuates bonding activities and helps repair these developmental gaps. Chapter 4 highlights the role of aggression, the nature-versus-nurture dilemma, the impact of learning on behavior, and the modeling of violence across generations. Here a dramatic client journey reveals not only the intensity of anger that can be repressed during

---

* Psychotherapists in the context of this book denote practitioners trained at the master's or doctoral level to treat mental, emotional, and behavioral disorders.

childhood illness and combat in Vietnam but also the transformation of repressed rage through the containing activity of shamanic beings.

Chapter 5 explores containment as furnished by both the journey and the psychotherapeutic process. It goes on to address alchemy, the activation of archetypal healing energy, and the archetypal shadow—repository of both individual and collective dysfunction. Deep within this shadow lies a bridge spanning the worlds of shamanism and psychology. In chapter 6 a rhythmic stride across this bridge sheds new light on the ego's maturation vis-à-vis the alchemy of shamanic healing. On the one hand, psychology becomes enriched by the infusion of spirit, and on the other, shamanism gains from theoretical possibilities. Collectively, they accelerate the healing of societal wounds.

Welcome to this journey. May your ride through its hills and valleys be relatively smooth. And may it expand the healing trail you are riding into the coming millennium.

Prologue

Shortly before my fifty-fifth birthday, as my marriage of thirty-two years was dissolving, I took a sabbatical from my psychology practice and moved to the country. To anyone who asked, I gave two reasons for this break in my professional activity: I wanted to spend time in South America and I wanted to reflect on my life. The latter desire dominated what turned out to be a hiatus of sixteen months, two of which were spent grappling with the Spanish language in Ecuador and Peru while being haunted by a disturbing unsettledness.

Prior to this period in my life, I had worked long and hard on troublesome aspects of my past. I had no doubt that emotional deficits and spiritual confusion had overshadowed my years of growing up in a German-Catholic family. And for some time I had suspected that my conscious mind did not grasp the entirety of the situation. When I returned from South America to a relatively remote area in northern New Mexico, there was little to interfere with the impact of isolation on my psyche; in the quiet of my small adobe house, the feel of my life began to resonate with the tenor of my childhood.

From the time of my earliest recollection I did not feel at home with my family. The contact I had with my parents, as well as with my many siblings, had little to do with how I felt deep inside. Something was missing; some vital part of me lay buried. I, more than the other children in my family, seemed to carry a sensitivity that left me with a gnawing sense of what psychoanalyst Michael Balint calls the "basic fault"—an essential flaw that keeps one in a state of emotional isolation and disconnectedness from those in the immediate environment. This feeling especially pervaded my relationship with my mother who, already burdened with five children by the time I was born, was diagnosed with cancer after the birth of the child four years my junior. She died when I was eight years old, leaving me no conscious memory of a mother's gentle touch or physical nurturing.

Balint attributes the origin of the basic fault to harsh, rigid, "ununderstanding," or indifferent modes of care in the formative period of infancy,[1] which may well have been my experience. My parents were pragmatic people ruled by hard work, stoicism, and concern about what others would think of them. Feelings were not articulated, affection was lacking, and teasing, put-downs, and dogmatism served as outlets for anger never openly expressed. I excelled in school and, when old enough, held as many jobs as I could after school hours to buy the things I wanted and to save money for college—which I saw as my ticket to a more meaningful and connected life. As a college student and on into early adulthood I managed to bring into my life people with whom I could feel some connectedness, although I often paid a caretaking price for it.

Middle-aged and living alone, I saw the pattern of my life stretching out before me in stark relief. Just as my childhood had not been able to support the emergence of a vital self, neither had my marriage. There was nowhere to turn but *inward* if I was to find answers to the questions that plagued me: Why, after all the psychological work I had done, was I feeling a despair that seemed to extend back in my life to long before the self-initiated ending of my marriage? What had happened to me other than the incidents I held in conscious memory?

Gradually, awarenesses surfaced. Startling dreams, the likes of which I had never before experienced, began to reveal their themes. And I came to understand the genesis of a rage that for decades had prowled along the periphery of my consciousness. My dreams, combined with the solitude of my life and countless hours of reflection, awakened within me a realization of abuse that carried physical and sexual overtones. This realization both relieved and overwhelmed me. Relieved me, because it validated my inner sense of something so inherently askew. Overwhelmed me, because it informed me of the truth of my experience. The initial torrent of feelings passing through me was bounded only by the hills into which I relentlessly hiked.

Something else happened during that first spring in the country. Traveling to a nearby mountain retreat site, I attended a weekend workshop conducted by a Native American medicine woman. Not knowing exactly why, I arranged to meet with her alone one morning the following week. It was a fortuitous meeting. Knowledgeable in shamanic ways, this woman of spiritual and natural strength breathed my first "power animal" into me. She lay on the floor next to me, went on a journey—that is, entered into a shamanic trance—and upon her return, knelt over me and blew the animal she had retrieved into my body. She instructed me not to reveal the nature of this animal to anyone. Furthermore, she advised me to begin "journeying" on my own once a week and to keep a written log of each experience. Never again did our paths cross.

My active involvement in shamanism began that day. My interest in shamanic phenomena, however, had been triggered years earlier. During graduate school I had taken a number of courses in cross-cultural psychology. At the same time, I was receiving training in Ericksonian hypnosis. Having discovered in my reading that trance states were natural occurrences in many cultures, I wondered how they induced psychological healing. On several occasions while working with individuals in a hypnotic state, I took note of the emergence of animals in trance imagery. But not until that memorable spring morning did I begin to understand the part they played.

I faithfully followed the medicine woman's suggestions. Once a week, while listening to the recorded beat of a drum, I moved through a tunnel in the earth and emerged into the natural setting of the "lower world." Here I interacted with my power animal, asking for instruction, protection, and strength. Were it not for my graduate school studies, my rational mind would surely have argued me out of what began to unfold.

Arriving in the lower world, I would see my power animal waiting for me. Sometimes I asked questions, and received answers either telepathically or by observing the animal's behavior. In response to a question I had about my future, the animal indicated that focusing on my present path was critical. Immediately, I felt a surge of healing energy move through my body. For five weeks the journeys, just short of a half hour each, offered me a respite from the pervasive emotional pain I awoke to each morning. Here in the journeying domain I found a sense of calm, softness, protection, and devotion.

My experience of the animal's commitment to my welfare strengthened with each encounter. Then in the sixth journey, a most profound event occurred. Arriving in the lower world, I was taken to a garden where I saw a circle of women caring for an infant—an infant I knew to be me. With loving tenderness, these women ministered to my infant-self. Journey after journey, I allowed myself to be touched and cared for in ways I had not experienced in infancy. Sometimes the women nurtured me in the garden; other times, angelic beings tended me in a clearing next to a rushing river. Always my power animal sat or lay next to me as a defender and benefactor of my well-being. In some instances the animal assumed a more active role, transmitting healing energy to parts of my body that had been abused.

I was not engaged in verbal therapy during these months. My intuition suggested that some kind of "containment," or holding, was taking place, the components of which were not to be articulated. Hence, I spoke of the details to no one. I did, however, allude to my newfound feelings of nurturance in weekly bodywork sessions, when the returning energy was compassionately and deftly secured into my body by the massage therapists attending me.

When I was about four months into journeying, my power animal made two brief appearances with the flesh of a lamb in its mouth. The lamb was dripping with blood, which I found curious, though not alarming. Months later I discovered that these two appearances were heralding another phase of work. Teeth and biting were by then familiar dream motifs. The devouring of lamb flesh, I realized, symbolized the violation of an innocent victim, an innocent *young* victim. A creeping dread began to surface as I saw where this work was taking me—straight to the grit of my buried rage.

I was knee-deep in a process I did not know how to *define* as a process. There had been no introductory lecture, no sales pitch, no planned outline, and no promise of recovery. What had felt like a fairly benign undertaking now gripped the core of my being and demanded that I pay attention.

Ensuing events helped to demystify some of this conundrum. To begin with, I read Sandra Ingerman's *Soul Retrieval.*[2] Partway through this book, I realized that my power animal, by leading me to my infant-self in the garden, had orchestrated my first soul retrieval experience. Soul retrieval, I learned, is the mission of a shamanic practitioner who, with the help of power animals or spirit beings (sometimes referred to as helping spirits), finds the lost part of an individual's soul and returns it to him.

Reading on, I found that soul loss, like its psychological counterpart, "dissociation," implies a splitting off of parts of the psyche as a result of trauma. Loss of this vital integrating energy manifests in such conditions as depression, memory loss, or addictive behaviors. Viewed psychologically, dissociation is a defense mechanism causing threatening feelings, impulses, or thoughts to be cast into the unconscious portion of the psyche. From the shaman's perspective, these split-off parts live in another dimension—a "nonordinary" yet parallel reality—and are accessible to those familiar with its topography.

Shamanic cultures, I found, understand the debilitating effects of trauma and strive to restore wholeness to distressed individuals. After an accident, major illness, death of a family member, or other misfortune, the shaman is summoned to bring back the missing part of the traumatized person. In the presence of family and community, she journeys into nonordinary reality and searches for the lost

portion of the person's soul. Upon finding it, she may need to con-
verse with it, offering assurance that in coming back it will be safe,
welcomed, and cared for. The shaman then returns with the "soul
essence" and blows it into the body of the waiting individual.[3]

I was heartened to learn that what to me had felt like a spontaneous experience with my infant-self was a shamanic technique that
had been in existence for hundreds of years. Suspecting that other
parts had been lost to me, I arranged to have a formal soul retrieval
by a shamanic practitioner. About the same time, I began attending
shamanic trainings sponsored by The Foundation for Shamanic
Studies. In these trainings additional power animals revealed themselves to me. I also learned to journey to another shamanic domain—
the "upper world"—where I encountered a spiritual teacher in human
form.

During the formal soul retrieval, which took place about eight
months after my first journey, several childhood parts were returned
to me. They ranged in age from three years to early adolescence,
indicating my age at the time of their respective departures. And
they each returned with feelings and impressions of painful events.
Realizing how many years had elapsed with so much of my vital
essence missing, I felt deeply sad. Then the sadness gave way to
rage. I envisioned the transgressed child who swallowed her anger
to ensure survival. No longer could my response to the pain and
loneliness be silenced.

The lamb that first appeared in the mouth of my power animal
was now in the body of a wolf who sought vindication. As surely as
I was starting to taste the rage in my mouth, I did not want to *feel* it.
No matter what frame of mind prevailed when I began a journey,
once in the presence of the upper world teacher, I became irritable.
To stave off the turmoil, I attempted to limit my journeys to the
lower world. This strategy did not work, for even there I began
experiencing extreme irritation. Whether I focused on the nurturing
activities of the lower world or the learning to be gleaned in the
upper world, the feeling tone of each journey reverted to the unexpressed rage of my child-self.

I figured I had one of two choices: to exit a journey prematurely (always an available option) or to own up to my frustration. Exiting, I discovered, was not a viable alternative, for I was not about to give up on this process that had effected so much healing. Owning up won out, though I remained reluctant to allow for the eruption of restrained feelings. The resistance I felt was immense. Then during a journey, one of the power animals conveyed a message that gave me pause: "It's OK to experience anything while journeying."

Vying with this message were powerful voices in my head warning me of the perils of anger. Echoes of parental and sibling injunctions, combined with the imprint of Catholicism, reminded me that angry thoughts, let alone angry feelings, were cause for a trip to the confessional. Reverberations of societal attitudes joined with Aquarian notions advising me that thoughts and feelings directed toward others could harm them. Consequently, I labored under the assumption that this journeying terrain, which I experienced as sacred, could become contaminated and perhaps nullified by the presence of antagonistic behaviors and attitudes.

I was enmeshed in an excruciating double bind: the child in me was trapped by a rage that sought to be released, while the parent in me forbade its expression. Why risk eternal damnation, I asked myself, when it seems "not that big a deal" to keep repressing what has heretofore been kept under wraps? My psychologist self knew better. I had taken particular note of a John Bradshaw imagery exercise in which the child-self invites the offending parents up on a stage, is given a sword, and proceeds to wield it against them while a "god-presence" gives witness to the action.[4] I was also aware of Harville Hendrix's container exercise that encourages the expression of anger by one spouse while the other sits in supportive witness of its release.[5]

Power animals are known for their humor and inventiveness, and mine were no exception. Shortly after I received the permission-giving message, another power animal escorted me from the lower world to the much avoided upper world. There was no escaping the wrath I felt.

The timing, however, could not have been better. Here in the realm of teachings, I began a series of lessons on acknowledging and releasing my anger. Toward that end, I was given a weapon and instructed to use it whenever an abusive figure appeared on the scene. Most often, the power animal in attendance arrived with a sword in its mouth, although one time it brought me a hatchet. Always, it patiently observed as I wielded these bladed instruments against my violators. Perhaps in witnessing my anger, these power animals would contain its energy and recycle it for other healing purposes, I reasoned. But this was just a seed of a thought, hardly capable of supplanting the staunch resistance that continued its hold on me. At the beginning of some journeys, I had to struggle to stay awake, sensing an irresistible pull to an unconscious state in which I would not have to feel the intensity of the anger—a fury I did not want to believe originated in me.

Each journey brought not only emotional discharge but physical release. My arms and legs quivered with the swinging of the sword or the ax. And my weekly visits to the massage team took on a new quality: the lightest touch to my body triggered anger. Just as the power animals were giving me supportive witness in the shamanic world, humans began offering compassionate witness to the outpouring of my fury in the massage room.

Interspersed among my upper world encounters were numerous visits to the lower world, where I was supported in interacting with the returned soul parts. Eventually these became integrated into my being, whereupon the number of nurturing journeys diminished. Likewise, the journeys of release reduced the rage dammed up inside me until they, too, decreased in frequency. I awakened to a new sense of self—a self with a greater ability to trust the world I lived in and the people I interacted with. Simultaneously, the concentrated internal experiences of healing gave way to a pursuit of learning from sources outside myself.

Two years into the shamanic experience, I traveled to the Cattaraugus Indian Reservation in upstate New York to engage in an intensive teaching from Twylah Nitsch. Grandmother Twylah, as she is affectionately called, is a Seneca elder and granddaughter of Moses Shongo, last of the great Seneca medicine men. Delving into the Seneca Cycles of Truth, I learned more about the teaching mission of my life and about the use of silence to deepen the understanding of inner truth.

Each training, each learning, and each journey I embarked on exposed me to more aspects of the world of unseen power and wisdom. I did not share my experiences with psychotherapy colleagues, however. My doctoral degree from a traditional program had been hard won, and my licensure as a psychologist awarded me credibility in a world I valued. I did not wish to be considered a marginal practitioner—an all too likely possibility in an area of the country known for alternative healing approaches that range from viably therapeutic to outright pretentious and uninformed.

In twenty-one years of consciously struggling to resolve my psychological dilemma, I had utilized many approaches—from traditional verbal therapy to consciousness-raising workshops, and from hypnosis and imagery to psychodrama—none of which afforded the healing power I experienced in the shamanic domain. The underlying depressive tenor to my existence gave way to an appreciation of life; waking in the morning was no longer shrouded in the silent dread of how loneliness and disconnection would play themselves out in the day before me. The belief that recurrent loss would dominate my life was replaced by contentment in relating with my children, grandchildren, and friends.

For me, journeying conferred a nurturance, validation, and emotional release not accorded in earlier developmental stages. Does this happen in traditional psychotherapy? I believe it does, although the process is typically long, arduous, and contingent on a level of skill and degree of therapeutic presence not found in every therapist. I also believe it sometimes unfolds independent of a structured therapeutic setting.

The return to my psychotherapy practice was gradual and part-time. Little by little I selectively incorporated shamanic approaches into my clinical work. All the while, I was mesmerized by questions that engaged my analytical mind: *How does the shamanic tradition bring such potent healing power to wounds incurred in the earliest months of life? Could journeying provide a release valve for the violence so rampant in our world?*

I hoped to find answers to the first question by examining the philosophical, historical, and methodological underpinnings of shamanism and psychology. The second question evoked fascination and more questions. Coming to terms with my own capacity for violent expression had sharpened my view of public displays of hostility. Aggression, I realized, deepens its imprint on our consciousness each time we see hatred in the eyes of a passing stranger or abuse heaped on a child in the marketplace. No longer is the propensity for violence relegated to the delinquent few, or even an "unspeakable" tendency peeking out from closets of the privileged and protected. *Countless* world citizens have grown up with the breath of violence hot and sultry on their necks. In the United States, violence is rising at a faster rate in the adolescent community than in any other sector of the population. And the number of homicides committed by younger children confounds our notion of childhood.

How is it possible to "turn the other cheek," I wondered, when there is no immunity against the epidemic of street and family violence? What does it mean to "do unto others as you would have them do unto you" when basic rights to life have not been granted? What are the prospects for four year olds who fear nuclear obliteration, worry about chemical crippling, or watch older siblings toting guns to school?

My hikes were crowded out by weekly visits to the library and daily treks through the stacks of books that began filling my study. Mounting excitement accompanied the discoveries I made while I read. In time a theoretical bridge emerged linking early developmental wounding with shamanic healing. I began to understand the role played by shamanic beings in filling the void left by developmental deprivation. I was able to see between the realms of shamanism and psychology a methodological meeting place rich with implications for redressing "acting-out behaviors." And so the book begins.

The Apple and the Orange

Imagine a psychologist holding an orange. Imagine a shaman holding an apple. The psychologist is planning to eat the orange with her lunch, after spending an hour in consultation with a client suffering from depression. While in session, she first queries her client about any side effects from the antidepressant prescribed by the attending physician. Then, applying a cognitive behavior model, she tracks progress on the treatment protocol: together, therapist and client review the client's log of dysfunctional thoughts and discuss ways to add more pleasurable activities to the weekly schedule. Role playing for improved assertiveness skills rounds out the hour. After the client leaves, the psychologist relaxes at her desk, peeling away the tough, resistant skin of the orange, eager to get to the succulent fruit inside.

The shaman drops the apple into his drum bag and heads for the household that has called for his services. Here, too, the client is depressed, and is surrounded by concerned and attentive family members. After appropriate greetings, the burning of incense and the lighting of candles set the stage for the shaman's drumming.

His movement into nonordinary reality and his interaction with power animals and spirit helpers culminate in an assessment of the client's condition; running his hands across her energy field, he learns that his charge is suffering from an intrusion of energy that he identifies as grief. He then removes the accumulation of stored grief by cupping his hands and scooping it from the patient's chest. To neutralize the effects of this misplaced energy, he directs it toward the nearest body of water. As the family members tend to their loved one with relief, the shaman moves silently into the night, happy to reach for the refreshment of the apple.

COMPARING SHAMANISM AND PSYCHOLOGY IS MUCH LIKE COMPARING AN apple and an orange. Their ideologies—like the colors, textures, and inner consistencies of the fruits—appear as oppositional as the popularly held notion that psychology is about science and shamanism is about superstition. Their purposes, however, are identical: both disciplines focus on the human condition and strive to alleviate suffering.

Shamanism, like the apple, has a core. This core is composed of beliefs, practices, apprenticeship requirements, and a symbology that are adhered to with remarkable consistency throughout the world. Uniting them all is the view that every bit of life is interrelated and that the world of spirit influences the world of matter. The universe is seen as alive, imbued with a creative essence that integrates all aspects of existence. The shaman taps into this spirit world by entering into an altered state of consciousness and embarking on a journey. He returns with information of benefit to his community.

Psychology, like the orange, has at its center a pithy axis surrounded by a number of segments. Although an underlying aim of conventional psychology is to establish itself as an *empirical* tradition grounded in measurement and evaluation, nowhere is there a nucleus of knowledge for today's students or practitioners to refer to. Rather, psychology is a hybrid discipline that encompasses an array of specialties ranging from experimental psychology to clinical psychology to neuropsychology, with dozens of specialties in between. Clinical psychology alone includes modes of treatment arising from psychoanalytic, behavioral, existential, and humanistic schools of thought.

Psychology is perhaps most analogous to the navel orange, a "double orange" bearing at its apex a small second fruit that does not develop. As in the double fruit, a secondary potential is inherent in psychology. This secondary expression is the *nonempirical* approach, and its lack of development poses a major predicament. The nonrecognition of soul beleaguers psychologists who subscribe to a belief in both the material and immaterial worlds; like others, I find myself aligning with one perspective one day and its opposite the next.

So we have, on the one hand, an apple that is thin-skinned and easy to sink one's teeth into, yet unduly susceptible to injury. Indeed, the tenets of shamanism are straightforward and readily accessible, whether or not we subscribe to them; but on its surface is a bruise, most likely resulting from the ease with which shamanism is discounted by analytically minded individuals. On the other hand, we have a thick nlrinned orange that appears uninviting and difficult to penetrate. Such is the nature of psychology—only after sifting though its potentially intimidating complexities can one appreciate the richness of its yield.

Given proper conditions, perhaps the embryonic second fruit of the "orange" can be activated, along with the ability of the "apple" to produce a more blight-resistant skin. After all, the acknowledgment of a spiritual essence does not have to weaken the scientific grounding of psychology. Nor would an analytical assessment of its procedures diminish the potency of shamanism.

Is some sort of "cross-pollination" possible? Can these two healing disciplines contribute anything of value to each other? While my own experience says yes, a theoretical understanding of where these arenas overlap, and how each can enrich the other, leads us to the definitions they give themselves and a look at the forces that shaped them.

Defining the Turf

The shaman's world, in all its flair, is reflected on the covers of books devoted to its many facets—showing kaleidoscopes of animals, dramatic fetishes, and mysterious landscapes exuding the surreal. However "otherworldly" its origins and manifestations may seem, shamanic practices have long existed in the most desolate to the most exotic places on the planet. The Russian nation of Tungus, in Siberia, for example, gave us the word *shamanism*, from its root word *šaman*, which denotes a person with spiritual power who is accomplished in the "technique of ecstasy," or journeying.[1] This technique of ecstasy, according to Mircea Eliade—the religious historian who coined the phrase in his classic text on shamanism—entails moving from normal consciousness into a state of magnified feeling and awareness. The soul of a shaman in this state leaves his body and travels to other realms of existence.

Unlike my first impression of the shaman's journey (an ethereal encounter with deities to which we ordinary mortals are not privy), the mission of journeying focuses on human concerns: "to acquire knowledge, power, and to help other persons."[2] Propelled by the belief that other beings, natural objects, and the universe itself are all endowed with vital essence or soul, the shaman attempts to communicate with these animate sources to obtain the information needed to alleviate suffering. In short, shamanism is a healing art. And the shaman is, in Eliade's words, "the great specialist in the human soul; he alone 'sees' it, for he knows its 'form' and its destiny."[3]

Psychology presents a far more conventional profile. In its most literal sense, psychology is defined as the study of the psyche, or mind. While the suffix *-logy* refers to a field of scientific study, *psyche* implies "breath" and, by way of extension, "life," "spirit," "human soul," or "mind."[4] In present-day psychology, however, the idea of spirit or soul is markedly absent; indeed, many texts now define psychology as the study of behavior and mental processes, and the application of knowledge to human functioning. So we see that implicit in the current definition of psychology is a denial of the existence of soul, or at least of any practical importance of soul in human behavior.

The Roots of Shamanism

The ancient tradition of shamanism appears to date back to Paleolithic times. Europe has the oldest evidence—animal skulls and bones believed to be shamanic ritual offerings found at sites inhabited between 50,000 and 30,000 B.C. The soundest evidence suggestive of shamanic practices came with the discovery of petroglyphs on the walls of prehistoric caves such as the Lascaux in France and the Altamira in Spain. Shamanic beings depicted in the Lascaux cave were engraved and painted in about 15,000 B.C. Here we find the figure of a "bird-headed man," indicative of flight and a capacity for the ecstatic journey;[5] profiles of deer, horses, cows, and bulls thought to be spirit helpers; and a unicorn figure sometimes interpreted as a "shaman in a skin" driving horses.[6] In 1994 a still older cave was unearthed in France. The Chauvet cave—replete with splendid drawings of horses, bison, rhinoceroses, lions, and an owl—is thought to date back more than 32,000 years.[7] These figures, too, suggest the presence of shamanic activity.[8] Whether viewed in books or on the walls of the museum that now stands close to the Lascaux cave (which is no longer open to visitors, due to an accelerated deterioration of its walls), these paintings all offer a breathtaking glimpse of life vivified by spirit.

The cave paintings tell one story; oral and written accounts reveal another. Much of what we know about shamanism comes from anthropologists, religious historians, and others who have visited indigenous cultures. These outsiders watched, listened, and recorded their observations, spicing them with the narratives of shamans themselves. Mircea Eliade, upon surveying a great deal of this information, found in documents based on widely diverse cultures certain common threads, including descriptions of the cosmic regions visited on ecstatic journeys.

The shaman's journeys take her to one of three destinations: a lower world, a middle world, and an upper world, all connected by a central axis. In this axis is an opening through which the gods come down to earth, the dead move to the underworld, and the shaman in her journey of ecstasy flies to the sky or descends into the subterranean realm.

This *lower world* (or underworld) is composed of natural settings resembling those found in our reality—earthy landscapes with forests, mountains, rivers, and deserts. Here the shaman interacts with the spirits of plants, trees, animals, and humans. Those "spirit beings" who take on animal forms are referred to as power animals. The *middle world* is the earth we live on, as perceived by the shaman while she journeys over it. In the *upper world* (or sky) the shaman receives teachings from beings of elevated or divine stature. When the intent of a journey—the procuring of healing information from these cosmic worlds—is fulfilled, the information is brought back and shared with others through prayer, dance, and ritual.

Shamanic activity has been observed worldwide, even in areas as remote as Oceania (three main groups of islands in the Pacific Ocean). According to Eliade, the most complete and most typical manifestation of shamanism has been in North and Central Asia. His description of shamanic activity in a Siberian region gives the flavor of a healing journey:

> When he is called to perform a cure, the Tremyugan shaman begins beating his drum and playing the guitar until he falls into ecstasy. Abandoning his body, his soul enters the underworld and goes in search of the patient's soul. He persuades the dead to let him bring it back to earth by promising them the gift of a shirt or other things; sometimes, however, he is obliged to use more forcible means. When he wakes from his ecstasy the shaman has the patient's soul in his closed right hand and replaces it in the body through the right ear.[9]

We would find strikingly similar beliefs and practices in any shamanic community we might visit. What accounts for these commonalities? It turns out that the passing on of shamanic traditions, unlike that of others, did not occur solely through the transference of information from generation to generation or from groups of people living close together. Other possibilities exist. Perhaps the migration of prehistoric civilizations from place to place contributed to the universality of core shamanic practices. Or perhaps an evolution of human consciousness galvanized by common needs, ideologies, mythologies, or religious intents evoked a collective expression.[10]

One of the universally practiced healing procedures issuing from the ecstatic state is *soul retrieval*. Here the shaman, like the Tremyugan healer described above, searches for the stricken person's soul, captures it, and returns it to the body. Another universal practice is *extraction*, a healing procedure in which the shaman diagnoses and removes energy foreign to the client's body, as is illustrated at the beginning of this chapter. The shaman may also take on the role of *psychopomp*, conducting a dead person's soul from the middle world to the lower world.

To be sure, the evolution of shamanism was influenced by outside forces. During the Middle Ages, for example, the intrusion of Buddhism and Lamaism into the ethnic groups of northern Asia shifted the shaman's focus from one supreme being to multiple divine beings and to increased communication with souls of the dead. Nevertheless, regardless of all the changes that occurred, "true shamanic ecstasy" as well as its healing purpose remains central to the integrity of shamanism as it is known today.[11]

A great deal of concern has been voiced worldwide about the waning practice of shamanism among indigenous people. Some say that shamanism is incompatible with many contemporary religions; others note that industrialization, life-style changes, high-tech advances, the drive toward specialization, and the development of economic systems favoring expedience and productivity have run roughshod over primitive and unproven practices. Whatever the cause may be for the decline in shamanic activity among indigenous people, there is another movement afoot: the beliefs and techniques of traditional shamanism have begun infiltrating Western thought and healing practices. Not only is a collective reconsideration of long-standing healing traditions occurring but deliberate attempts to ensure their survival are increasing. A prime example is the work taking place at The Foundation for Shamanic Studies (FSS) headed by anthropologist Michael Harner. Based in California, the FSS teaches core shamanic practices to interested students of all backgrounds and works toward the preservation and revival of shamanism among indigenous peoples.

Is Shamanism a Religion?

Eliade, no doubt, would answer yes to this question. From outward appearances, however, shamanism does not *look* like a religion. Devoid of conventional trappings of religion as we know it, shamanism has no catalog of doctrines or index of moral declarations, no buildings honoring its deities, no prayer assignments for congregants, and no hierarchy of power. Nor does it impart devotion to a messianic cause. What it does impart is a belief in many gods and spirits, as well as faith in the actions and narratives inspired by this belief.

Can such a grounding be called "religious"? According to university religion professor Åke Hultkrantz, it can. "Since the supernatural world is the world of religion," he states, "shamanism plays a religious role."[12]

Amid the recent upsurge of interest in shamanism, a more secularized interpretation of its practices has emerged, including that of Hungarian researcher Mihály Hoppál:

> Shamanism is a complex system of beliefs which includes the knowledge of and belief in the names of helping spirits in the shamanic pantheon, the memory of certain texts (sermons, shaman-songs, legends, myths, etc.), the rules for activities (rituals, sacrifices, the technique of ecstasy, etc.) and the objects, tools and paraphernalia used by shamans (drum, stick, bow, mirror, costumes, etc.). All these components are closely connected by beliefs given in the shamanic complex. . . . [Shamanism is] an overtly altruistic ideology which, in our egoistic and materialistic times, contains a decisively positive program for life.[13]

Hence it appears that shamanism both is and is not a religion. It stands apart from institutionalized religion, yet participates in an ancient mystical tradition that author John Lash describes as "perhaps the oldest form of practical spirituality in the world."[14]

The lens has also shifted in regard to the shaman's function. In early tribal societies, the shaman performed many roles, including medicine man or woman, priest or priestess, and sorcerer. Over time, these functions became more distinct and highly specialized. Medicine men and women were needed to oversee the treatment of certain illnesses requiring herbs and other medicinals; priests and priestesses were called upon to perform religious rites by offering prayers and sacrifices; and sorcerers and witches were sought out for their expertise in magic.

Presently, the terms "shaman" and "medicine man" or "medicine woman" are no longer interchangeable, nor are labels such as "intermediary" or "magician" accurate descriptions of a shaman. True, the shaman may exercise a variety of faculties: she practices magic while attempting to exert control over the forces of nature, functions as a medium while interacting with spirits, and may also serve as the medicine woman in her community. But her means of execution is different from those of her counterparts, for she relies on the technique of ecstasy. This voluntary use of an altered state of consciousness, combined with the intent to serve the community, sets shamanism apart from all other expressions of healing, mediumship, or sorcery.[15, 16]

The Initiation Process

The path to becoming a shaman has been depicted in many movies over the past several decades. While such fictionalized versions of this phenomenon may well constitute an invasion of sacred territory, they offer glimpses into an extraordinary process that staggers Western comprehension. These films, in keeping with material described in the literature, portray an initiation challenge beset by overwhelming demands, no matter how the summons occurs. Some initiates inherit the mission through lineage; others are "called" through dreams and visions; still others set forth by choice. Genetic transmission and direct bidding from the gods and spirits are said to convey the most power. As for gender, shamans are either male or female, although historically, most have been men.

Regardless of mode of entry or gender, a candidate is not considered a shaman until two types of learning have been mastered. The first comes through either the ecstatic experience or dreams. Initiatory themes often include a descent to the lower world, where the candidate speaks with souls of dead shamans, and an ascent to the upper world, where he communes with divine beings. During these encounters, which may coincide with a period of fast and isolation, he learns about the shamanic vocation. Perhaps the most enlightening of these lessons comes with a symbolic death and resurrection, in which the initiate's body is dismembered and then restored to wholeness with the aid of spirit beings. The second type of learning the initiate must undergo calls for instruction in techniques, symbolic language, and the genealogy of the clan as transmitted by the old tribal shamans.[17]

The unfolding of each initiation is different. In some, the initiate experiences a progressive change in behavior, during which he isolates himself and surrenders to an internal focus through meditation, dreams, and trances. In others, the initiation proceeds from an illness or near-death experience. Both the inner reflection and the self-healing elicit help from spirits that will later assist the individual in healing others. These spirits may be either divine "god" beings or more familiar beings called guardian or helping spirits.[18]

The divine beings are from the realm of the deities and are considered extremely powerful. They are not as accessible as guardian spirits, which often take the form of animals and perhaps account for the animal-like behavior emblematic of the shaman. While imitating the actions and intonations of one of these spirits, the shaman is thought to be "possessed" by the animal. To an outsider witnessing such a scene, another thought may arise: Has the shaman gone berserk?

The Psychological Status of the Shaman

Shamans, according to some anthropologists, are deranged, exhibiting symptoms of hysteria, hallucinations, "epileptic seizures," and schizophrenic episodes when they journey; they see visions, dance, or fall to the ground and emit primitive sounds. At least two heavyweight shamanic experts think differently—among them, Eliade. He strongly defended the psychological health and integrity of the shaman, pointing out that the trance state is under the shaman's command and is entered into at will, as are the actions and sounds of ecstatic activity. Furthermore, he commented, the degree of mental concentration and physical stamina called for in the ecstatic state is extraordinary and could not be endured by individuals of weak mind or faint heart.[19]

The trouble with anthropologists of the past, anthropologist and psychiatrist Roger Walsh tells us, is that they were often culturally biased, and that even today they are not trained in the diagnosis and evaluation of pathological states. Perceptions of most visitors, he adds, have been molded by Western psychiatry, the official diagnostic organ of mental health in our society, which until recently, categorized religious experiences and states of altered consciousness as pathological.

Walsh reminds us that the culture in which activity is observed is of pivotal importance when classifying behaviors. In shaman-based communities the ecstatic journey calls forth esteem, which is a far cry from the discomfort and disdain prompted by schizophrenic displays in our culture. The journey is entered into at will, as opposed to dissociative states such as hysteria, which "appear to overtake and control their victims."[20] Furthermore, the purpose of the shaman's journey is to open to pain—either his own or that of the sufferer—in order to bring about healing, whereas dissociative states facilitate the avoidance of pain.

What about the peculiar behaviors of the shaman in training? First of all, the shamanic initiate is in a spiritual crisis precipitated by an apparition of danger or a serious illness. Hence, in the early stages of initiation the candidate may appear overtaken by the process. Besieged by spirits, tormented, transported to the upper world and underworld, and subjected to the rite of dismemberment, he may exhibit pathological symptoms reminiscent of hallucinations, delusions, and depersonalization. Dialogues with animals, souls of dead shamans, and deities may also erupt in this period of seclusion from his community and deprivation of food and comfort.

Eliade has recounted the following experience of a Siberian Tungus initiate:

> [A] Tungus shaman relates that [in the early stages of initiation] he was sick for a whole year. During that time he sang to feel better. His shaman ancestors came and initiated him. They pierced him with arrows until he lost consciousness and fell to the ground; they cut off his flesh, tore out his bones and counted them; if one had been missing, he could not have become a shaman. During this operation he went for a whole summer without eating or drinking.[21]

Walsh concedes that the behavior of a shamanic candidate can give the appearance of a psychotic episode, but states that it could imply a "brief reactive psychosis" or an "atypical psychosis." He emphasizes that this behavior distinguishes itself from most psychiatric disorders by the brevity of the episode and the fact that it both occurs in response to an overwhelming situation and appears to result in complete recovery. Walsh states:

> Native peoples often make sharp distinctions between shamanic crises and mental illness. Moreover, shamans often seem to end up not only psychologically healthy but exceptionally so. This is in marked contrast to schizophrenics, many of whom deteriorate progressively over the years.[22]

The maturing of the initiate into a healer of substance and soundness is integral to the shamanic tradition. Consequently, the initiatory process, replete as it is with pathological elements, is considered too complicated a course of instruction to be integrated by anyone who is emotionally or mentally compromised.

Each time the initiate overcomes challenging forces by willingly entering into spiritual or mystical dimensions previously unknown to him, and by marshaling his internal resources with the aid of spirit helpers, he grows in shamanic strength. The day then comes when he will demonstrate his ability to communicate with these helping spirits by choice—to set aside his everyday sense of self and invoke the assistance of a helping spirit by imitating its actions and sounds, wearing masks suggestive of its appearance, and dancing its essence.

The ease with which the shaman abandons his body and moves from one realm to another is the symbolic scepter of healing he brings to his people. For him, the psychic integrity of the community is sovereign, which is why he serves to protect it against disease and demons. "It can be said that shamanism defends life, health, fertility, the world of 'light' against death, diseases, sterility, disaster and the world of 'darkness,'" Eliade tells us.[23]

The shaman is first and foremost a healer. Yet incidents of charlatanism, professional posturing, trickery, and deceit can and do crop up. Shamanic chronicles refer to instances in which shamans have capitalized on a client's belief that a cure is in the making, taking advantage, no doubt, of the widely known placebo effect. Though shamans—like psychotherapists, physicians, and religious leaders—may misuse their powers or lapse into self-deception, the consensus regarding their endurance, devotion to healing, and successful outcomes points to shamanism as a phenomenon to be reckoned with. It is of particular significance today, when increasing numbers of individuals are seeking the effects of holistic healing methods.

The Roots of Psychology

Whether we endorse it or not, shamanism excites our imaginations, resonating with the right side of the brain, where creativity, intuition, spontaneity, and even healing capacities are said to reside. Psychology, on the other hand, activates a shift to the left brain, where the capacity for chronology and reason come into play. For most of us Westerners, delving into the history of a field that was birthed out of Greek philosophy is more familiar—and often, far more comfortable. Here we gravitate toward things we can ultimately measure and justify. Here, too, we discover a curious circularity when we trace the beginnings of philosophy from ancient Greece to the questions posed by present-day psychologists. Let's take a closer look at these perennial ponderings.

Philosophical Moorings

Well over 2,000 years ago, the ancient Greeks were the first people to ask what the world was made of and why it is the way it is. These cosmologists reacted to the superstitious and magical practices of earlier civilizations, energizing a philosophical dance that has pirouetted for centuries between materialism and spiritualism. The dance began as cosmologists witnessed people relating to everything in nature as if it were alive (animism) and projecting human attributes onto nature's landscape (anthropomorphism). For these people, rocks and trees contained souls and the sky and earth expressed feelings through thunder, lightning, and volcanic eruptions. Cosmologists found shamanic healing approaches as suspect as attempts to appease the gods through sacrifice and magic.

These early Greek philosophers strove to replace supernatural explanations with natural ones. They looked for "the one substance" from which everything is derived—covering all the bases from water, earth, fire, and air to mathematical constancies and the boundless space of the universe.[24] Although they failed to find their sought-for substance, they demonstrated that the existence of varying beliefs provides endless fodder for debates and evaluations, warming us to the idea that truth is forever in the making. These philosophers also probed the meaning of life and the purpose of human existence, setting the stage for psychological thinking. They wanted to know, for example: *Is human behavior governed by physical factors alone or by a spiritual essence as well?*

Aristotle's response made history. Like his predecessors Socrates and Plato, he believed in the existence of a soul, asserting that the "active reason" part of the soul propels humanity toward its highest purpose—the acquisition of knowledge. His ideas, expressed in the fourth century B.C., are considered the most significant contributions to the field of psychology prior to the seventeenth century.[25, 26] Indeed, his theory of the human being's inner potential is considered a forerunner of self-actualization theory, reflected in the twentieth-century approaches of Carl Jung and of Abraham Maslow, a champion of humanism. About seven centuries after Aristotle's response, church father St. Augustine confirmed the validity of introspection, believing that scrutiny of one's inner experiences provides a vehicle for personal communion with God.

Early Greek philosophers, in other words, proposed that human existence has meaning and that the human mind can guide us in the right direction, suggesting that perhaps we really can measure "the one substance"! Such a state of affairs was destined to succumb to human complexity, and that it did, with the arrival of the Renaissance. Enter René Descartes, the father of modern philosophy and modern psychology, whose primacy of the mind—"I think, therefore I am"—separated mind from matter, allocating to each one its own set of principles. Some of his followers focused on his theory of body functions and envisioned human beings as mere machines with actions conveniently mechanized. Others accepted Descartes's belief in a soul that could be understood only through reflection. The notion of mind and body as separate yet interactive survives today and contributes to the tug-of-war between alternative and traditional approaches to healing.

As philosophers continued to contemplate the nature and workings of the universe, psychologists turned their attention to the *mechanics of consciousness and behavior.* The industrial revolution, along with scientific advances of the last century, further shaped psychology into a separate discipline. Indeed, science proved to be a perfect companion to legitimatize this offspring of philosophy! Empiricism, which contends that all knowledge comes from sensory experience and is based on objective facts discovered through observation and experimentation, had cast its spell.

By the late nineteenth century, experimental psychology had been launched; and by the turn of the twentieth century, the spiritual influences forming the early warp and woof of psychology's philosophical fabric were on the decline. In France and the United States, psychologists were attempting to measure intelligence. In Russia, Ivan Pavlov was working with conditioned and unconditioned reflexes. In Germany, Wilhelm Wundt was striving to link physiology with mental processes. Nonetheless, spirituality was not completely in the closet. In fact, Harvard psychologist William James, who had studied all aspects of behavior, maintained that any belief contributing to a more effective life was of value, be it scientific or religious.

These early decades of scientific psychology were known as the "era of the schools," but none discovered the unifying paradigm psychologists yearned for—a deficit that continues to plague the profession.[27] Psychology, as we know it, remains a collection of approaches, each struggling to find a comfortable niche somewhere between empiricism and humanism.

Twentieth-Century Influences

The twentieth century brought heady times to those invested in theoretical and methodological explosions in psychology. Some approaches have already had their heyday, whereas others are just coming into their prime, and still others are being recycled—either revived and woven into newer notions or better yet, evolving naturally out of older ones. As we look at the more predominant influences of this century, take note of the ambiguity in the way psychology defines itself with respect to the presence or absence of soul.

Behaviorism. More than any other approach, behaviorism sought to make psychology an empirical science capable of predicting and controlling behavior. Founded in the United States by John B. Watson in the early 1920s, behaviorism conjures up images of food-deprived rats running through mazes, dogs salivating to the reverberations of tuning forks, and people conditioned through pain, as depicted in the movie *Clockwork Orange*. Behaviorists' explanations of human behavior rarely took into account what was going on in the mind. Researchers focused instead on measuring environmental conditions and subjects' responses to them. Mention of soul or spirit was anathema.

Findings from other fields of science, such as ethology and genetics eventually helped to soften behaviorism's focus on environmental influences. In addition to studying physiological functioning and developmental phases, modern experimental psychologists have turned their attention to such cognitive processes as language, thinking, perception and memory, and other *internal* causes of behavior.

One of the splinter groups that has appeared in the wake of behaviorism is information-processing cognitive psychology, in which the brain is likened to a computer. Researchers in this field are attempting to create artificial intelligence by designing machines capable of replicating the intelligent behavior of living organisms. Philosophical and ethical concerns mount as we wonder if such soul-threatening advances bypass freedom of choice and the exercise of free will. The seemingly new questions triggered by artificial intelligence are actually the original ones posed when psychology was still tethered to its philosophical roots: *What is the nature of the mind? How do we learn?*

Psychoanalysis. One hundred years after Sigmund Freud presented psychoanalysis to the world, his name remains a conversational byword. His far-reaching influence reflects, in part, his ability to synthesize the philosophical ideas of others—among them, Johann Wolfgang von Goethe, Friedrich Wilhelm Nietzsche, and Karl Hartmann, who wrote a book entitled *Philosophy of the Unconscious*.[28] As Freud observed his patients and evaluated their cases, he crystallized the concepts he had studied into a theory of personality, describing it as an energy system that seeks to maintain equilibrium between forces emanating from three parts of the psyche—the id, ego, and superego.

Psychoanalysis explains both normal and abnormal behavior, the concept of unconscious motivation, the influence of childhood experience on adult functioning, and the role of defense mechanisms. But what kind of yardstick do you use to measure the unconscious, and how do you capture a morsel of psychological denial or projection for microscopic study? Such tasks are impossible, and consequently, psychoanalysis suffers as a scientific model. Furthermore, it has taken a bad rap from some quarters for not advancing the notion of a spiritually endowed psyche. This critique, however, was contested by child psychologist Bruno Bettelheim, who maintained that English translations of Freud's works *eliminated references to soul*.[29] While it is true that Freud considered religion an illusion that kept people in an infantile state, his understanding of spirit is another matter and will be left to the experts to unravel.

Almost from the beginning, Freud's theory was criticized for its deterministic view of human nature and its emphasis on sexual motivation. Carl Jung, one of several who broke with the psychoanalytic ranks, redefined many Freudian concepts and presented a more optimistic, creative view of humankind. To Jung, the libido was a pool of energy to be tapped for positive growth, rather than simply a reservoir of sexual energy. In addition, as mentioned earlier, he introduced into modern psychology Aristotle's idea of self-actualization, and did so with spiritual nuances.

For many years, Jung's school of thought was rejected by mainstream psychologists because of its emphasis on clinical examples and its historical and mythical leanings. "Jung has far less appeal than Freud," personality theorists Calvin Hall and Gardner Lindzey wrote in 1978, "because there is so much discussion of occultism, mysticism, and religion in Jung's writings that it apparently repels many psychologists."[30] The consensus changed, however, over the last twenty years. Jungian analysts began to garner respect, while Jung's use of symbols, dream interpretation, and active imagination were adopted by countless psychotherapists. The impact of Jung's ideas about the collective unconscious and archetypes soon permeated Western culture. Today, Jungian psychology is credited with thrusting psychological thought into the realm of the soul.

Third Force Psychology. Compared with the currents evident in the first half of the twentieth century, the wind blew in from a different direction in the 1960s, a phenomenon that made its mark on psychology with the upswell of existentialism and humanism. The similarities in these two approaches gave rise to the label "existential-humanistic psychology," abbreviated to "humanistic psychology" or "third force psychology." Both *humanistic psychology* and *existential psychology* uphold the importance of free will; authenticity; accepting responsibility for one's actions; acknowledging the uniqueness of human beings; studying the human being as a whole; exploring subjective experience; and seeking a meaningful life through personal growth. But whereas humanists (seeing human nature as fundamentally good) underscore the capacity for fulfillment and social responsiveness, existentialists (viewing human nature as neutral) focus on freedom of choice as a vehicle for bringing meaning to individual existence.[31] This difference sometimes plays itself out in humanists displaying a more optimistic outlook toward life.

Abraham Maslow originated humanistic psychology, and his emphasis on individual potential set third force psychology apart from behaviorism and the analytic approaches. Rather than scrutinizing symptomatic patients, he studied healthy, creative people and constructed a motivational framework based on what he called "a hierarchy of needs." When physiological, safety, belonging, and self-esteem needs are met, he theorized, an individual is better able to achieve self-actualization—that is, to reach his full human potential.

Maslow did not stop here, however. He went on to incorporate organismic theory into his perspective, taking the philosophical pitch to a higher octave. Organismic theory was first publicized in 1926 by Jan Smuts, in his book *Holism and Evolution*. Smuts, who created the word *holism* from the Greek root *holos*—meaning complete, whole, or entire—presented the human organism not as an outgrowth of mind and body, each with its own driving forces, but as a unified, integrated, and coherent entity motivated by one sovereign drive toward self-realization.[32] Third force psychology, in turn, spotlighted humankind's search for meaning and our

built-in capacity for growth, relegating behaviorism's environmental influences to the bleachers. True understanding of a
human being (an organism distinct from an animal studied in a
laboratory), according to third force psychologists, could only
come from studying the *entirety* of the individual, since everything is related to the whole.

In short, rather than focusing on symptoms, Maslow and his
colleagues viewed their clients through a lens of possibility
framed by self-knowledge and self-responsibility. Movement
toward wholeness encompassed the role played by spiritual influences and experiences, and Maslow's hierarchy of needs embod-
ied mystical, or peak, experiences—moments of self-actualization
during which an individual feels more integrated, more at one
with the world, more perceptive, and more creative. In his words,
"The emotional reaction in the peak experience has a special flavor of wonder, of awe, of reverence, of humility and surrender
before the experience as before something great."[33]

Here we have another psychological approach that, like psychoanalysis, does not lend itself to empirical evaluation. Some say
the third force perspective has more in common with religion and
philosophy than with psychology. Yet, the existentialists within its
own ranks take offense at any mention of a spiritual component
underlying psychology (after all, the existentialist Nietzsche said
that God was dead).

Spiritual debates aside, one outcome is certain: holism, as
adopted by third force psychologists in their emphasis on the
whole person, eclipses Descartes's dualism. The mind-body split
cannot survive holism which, as Smuts described it, "[explains]
both the realism and the idealism at the heart of things, and is
therefore a more accurate description of reality than any of these
more or less partial and one-sided world views."[34] The assertion
that the world is not composed entirely of mind or matter—or the
interaction of the two *or* the coexistence of both—brings us to the
acknowledgment of a single organizing force. In other words spirit, or soul, already heralded by Jung, reenters the picture from yet
another camp.

Transpersonal Psychology. The wind that ushered in third force psychology wasn't finished blowing, for in the late 1960s transpersonal, or fourth force, psychology, sprang forth from the womb of third force psychology. Abraham Maslow wasn't finished with his endeavors either, for he had become a member of this newly fledged group that wanted to move beyond the boundaries of the actualizing self into dimensions of the obscure and psychologically forbidden. Transpersonal psychologists sought to probe eight categories of experience: states of consciousness; unity and the cosmic; being, essence, and ultimate meaning; transcendence; spirit; meditation; interpersonal or intrapersonal focus; and transpersonal actualization and realization.[35]

This, you might say, was a wind of many directions blowing in a wide variety of practitioners, including a cadre not trained within the bounds of psychology and counseling. Especially appealing to the spiritually oriented therapists filling these ranks was the incorporation of holism as well as Maslow's concept of the peak experience. Offsetting this optimistic focus on human potential, however, has been the lack of attention paid to the shadow side of human existence.[36] Nonetheless, vested as it was in spirituality and unity, fourth force psychology marked its point of departure from existential psychology to concentrate on the upper region of Maslow's hierarchy of needs. Consequently, increased consideration is now being placed on states of consciousness outside ordinary awareness.[37]

Many psychologists attribute this state of affairs to the blowing of an ill wind. Numerous scientific-minded clinicians and researchers are raising questions: *How can we legitimize efforts to address the unquantifiable and nonreproducible events? How can we endorse what cannot be objectively verified?* Transpersonal psychologists reply: *How can we NOT grapple with the characteristics of consciousness? After all, just because we can't measure it does not mean it doesn't exist.*

The Contemporary Picture

We are presently back where we began, wrestling with the dilemma that plagued the early Greek philosophers. Only now, this age-old quandary divides psychology into two cultures: empiricists who work toward scientific validation and humanists who explore human values, including those pertaining to the notion of a soul.[38] The scant regard given by conventional psychology to the work of nonempirical investigators, such as Jung, arouses concern that in its pursuit of a scientific identity, psychology will lose all contact with its philosophical roots. Historian Daniel Robinson points out that from the third through the seventeenth centuries, psychological writing consistently dealt with spiritual matters, but that "since 1930, there has not been a major psychological work expressing a need for spiritual terms in an attempt to comprehend the psychological dimension of man."[39] Evidently, Robinson does not credit Jung with mainstream status. Still, his point is well taken; the greatest misgiving for Robinson and others is that *the spiritual nature of human beings may be lost from psychology's official landscape.*

On a brighter note, if the ratio of practitioners specializing in clinical versus academic or experimental psychology is any indication of an investment in humanistic over scientific values, humanism is gaining momentum. Over the past two decades, clinical and counseling practitioners have come to comprise about 50 percent of all doctoral- and master's-level psychologists; over the same period of time the percentage of research psychologists has dropped. Moreover, in the general population more people than ever before now think of a psychologist as one who treats clients suffering from mental health problems rather than one who toils in a laboratory testing rats.[40]

In addition, the borders between different theoretical approaches are blurring. Jungians are now studying developmental stages while Freudians are learning cognitive techniques to aid in the treatment of depression. The recent introduction of Eye Movement Desensitization and Reprocessing (EMDR) is attracting enthusiasts of every persuasion. Activated from a behavioral background and allowing for objective measurement, EMDR is said to access a natural processing network that moves information in the brain to an adaptive resolution—movement that may involve the surfacing of unconscious material.[41] This method is far removed from those devised in the pioneering decades of behaviorism, and is perhaps a step closer to the acceptance of a soul.

Other pots boil on the stove. Neuroscientist Karl Pribam and physicist David Bohm offer theories on the holographic nature of the brain, stating: "Our brains mathematically construct 'concrete' reality by interpreting frequencies from another dimension, a realm of meaningful, patterned reality that transcends time and space. The brain is a hologram, interpreting a holographic universe. . . . Any piece of the hologram will reconstruct the entire image."[42] Surely, a true understanding of the holographic paradigm requires study, yet here we have scientists exploring what many people regard as "supernatural phenomena."

Science and philosophy, it seems, are eyeing each other with curiosity, perhaps even courting each other. In a 1994 *Scientific American* article entitled "Can Science Explain Consciousness?" the long-standing debate between philosophy and science seems to have lost its footing, even though the question of who bears the responsibility for explaining consciousness comes to no definitive conclusion. Holistic physician Andrew Weil suggests that whoever attempts to move toward an understanding of consciousness must deal with reports that indigenous people of South America experience identical hallucinations after ingesting psychedelic drugs.[43] Does this observable phenomenon fall within the domain of science or philosophy? And to which does psychology belong?

Psychologists, alas, do not know. Despite the professional and societal shifts going on within and around it, psychology remains politically deadlocked. The discipline appears to have assimilated humanistic perspectives with relative ease, but its most important official voice, the American Psychological Association (APA), withholds sanction from psychologists who pursue the study of states considered paranormal, religious, or transcendent. Whereas humanistic psychology holds membership in the APA, transpersonal psychology has not succeeded in its bid for acknowledgment. It is criticized for focusing too much upon "otherworldliness" and for going "beyond humanness."[44] All the same, the empiricists' struggle for scientific legitimacy has yet to be won, and according to some historical commentators, may never be won. Why? Because psychology, unlike other disciplines, still has the most enigmatic questions to answer—namely, *Why are we what we are? And why do we do what we do?*[45]

Historians of psychology conclude their discussions of the current predicament with provocative musings. Daniel Robinson declares psychology to be the history of ideas.[46] And B. R. Hergenhahn asserts:

> It seems that psychology is not a place for people with a low tolerance for ambiguity. . . . There is growing recognition that psychology must be as diverse as the humans whose behavior it attempts to explain. . . . For those willing to ponder several truths, psychology is and will continue to be an exciting field.[47]

Will psychology incorporate the ambiguity and diversity? If not, we might witness harvests from two (or more) fields of psychology.

Common Ground between Shamanism and Psychology

The purpose of shamanism is to heal. The function of psychology is to study behavior and mental processes, and to apply the resulting knowledge to the human condition. Shamanism employs supernatural practices to achieve its purpose. Psychology, in many of its branches, relies on rational and scientific means to fulfill its objectives. Yet, regardless of their differences, both shamanism and psychology seek to alleviate suffering in communities of people.

In addition to sharing this healing intent, the segments of psychology that embrace spiritual or supernatural elements—namely, third force, fourth force, and Jungian approaches—share a good deal of common ground with shamanism. The self-actualizing variant of third force psychology is a case in point. Peak experiences, those self-actualizing moments in which feelings of unity and sacredness prevail, can happen to anyone, but are most frequently reported by individuals at the spiritual end of Maslow's hierarchy of needs. Such experiences sometimes provide an understanding of the "whole of Being," accompanied by a transformative shift in which the individual begins to see reality as either neutral or good, framing evil as "only a partial phenomenon" of the whole. This universal perspective can prompt a reconciliation with pain and death.[48] Here we are reminded of the initiate's encounter with her own finiteness and vulnerability, which forces her to muster previously untapped energies and strengths that promote a more integrated sense of self.

Both the peak experience and the initiate's journey involve a transcendence of natural law and lead to godlike states or contact with beings described as expansive and enriching. Both events are also ego transcending. The peak experience overcomes self-consciousness as the individual's perceptions organize around a different reality. The shaman who is called upon to minister to a sick individual leaves her ego at the threshold of nonordinary reality before embarking on an ecstatic journey in which alternate reality is as real as ordinary reality, and in which she encounters beings wiser than herself.

Other similarities also exist. Peak experiences are associated with highly actualized individuals, as is the ecstatic journey; the shaman is said to display a higher than average degree of psychological integrity. Self-actualizing individuals, compared with those who are not, identify more strongly with humankind, displaying more tolerance and compassion for the pain and misfortune of others. Likewise, the shaman's devotion to the health of her community springs from a highly developed capacity to confront the maladies of those in her care with equanimity and impartiality, a task for which she has been purified by her own initiatory crisis.

In at least five of the eight areas of experience investigated by transpersonal psychologists, fourth force psychology shares additional territory with shamanism. The shaman moves into a different *state of consciousness* when she journeys, experiences *transcendence* as she enters the *unified cosmic* domains of the shamanic world, and communes with *spirit* in her pursuit of healing information. Furthermore, during her initiatory crises, she undergoes an *intrapersonal* metamorphosis.

Holism—a perception of the world as governed by a creative organizing force and knowing no separation between mind and matter—underscores approaches of the shaman, the humanist, and the transpersonalist. Relating to any part of this universe in the context of its wholeness activates physical, mental, emotional, and spiritual dynamics adding up to much more than the sum of each of the parts. A healer, whether shamanic or holistic, regards a client's symptoms in terms of his entire beingness *and* within the context of his environment and circumstances.

Finally, shamanism and psychology meet behind a veil lifted by Carl Jung when he portrayed a supernatural world never before displayed in the psychological literature. His descriptions of archetypes, alchemy, and the role of the unconscious allow us to understand what happens within the client when the shaman enters the shamanic domain: as the shaman drums, archetypes arise from the unconscious, transforming the psyche's fractures into mended wholes.

From the outside, psychologists appear divided over the concept of shamanism. The humanist, transpersonal, and Jungian segments of psychology, which endorse a world imbued with spirit, tend to be at home with shamanic practices, whereas the empirical segments cast aside this ancient tradition, branding it unscientific and illogical. The truth of the matter is that as psychologists of all persuasions go about their healing and research many, either knowingly or unknowingly, employ shamanic-like techniques.

So it appears that with a mind-set bent on distinguishing the "apple" from the "orange," one cannot perceive that their sizes, shapes, hues, and essences are actually quite similar. A holistic perspective, on the other hand, opens us to such a perception, all the while enriching our appreciation of these two healing disciplines.

Shared Slices

*It's another day. The shaman and the psychologist meet beneath a
tree and sit down together. The psychologist slices her orange with
a knife and hands it to the shaman, who proceeds to cut the apple.
They then share slices of fruit, the psychologist appreciating the
crispness of the apple as the shaman savors the juice of the orange.*

*It does not seem to matter that in their professions the psychologist
calls upon the intellect while the shaman invokes supernatural
forces. The two have come together because they know of their shared
intent to heal. But do they also know that their traditions share
related approaches and methodologies? Do they know that the nature
of the healing relationship, the use of altered states of consciousness
and imagery, as well as the function of the unconscious play major
roles in the healing endeavors they each engage in?*

HEALING HAPPENS. IT HAPPENS WHETHER OR NOT WE BELIEVE IN SOUL.
What's more, healing comes in varying guises and assumes many
names: the heart surgeon replaces a valve, the physical therapist
rehabilitates a broken leg, the *curandera* applies herbs, the psy-

41

chotherapist helps process thoughts and feelings, and the shaman retrieves lost essence. Common to each approach are specific characteristics of healing. First, a *sufferer* seeking relief from an ailment or disturbance solicits the assistance of a *healing agent* trained in curative skills and regarded as effective. The two then form a *healing relationship,* and during one or more sessions the healer attempts to bring relief to the sufferer.

The sort of relief the healing agent offers depends on his training. A therapist, drawing on the *rhetorical* approach that originated in the oratories of ancient Greece, implements aspects of drama, philosophy, or persuasion. He also makes use of the *empirical* tradition, which dates back to Hippocrates' systematic study of the human body, calling on structured and tested methods to restore well-being. A shaman, associated with a *religiomagical* tradition, believes in supernatural forces as the cause and cure of illness. His interaction with beings in nonordinary reality procures healing information that he then uses to soothe his charge.[1]

Despite these differences, healing relationships in psychology and shamanism share universal elements. Initially, the degree to which a "meeting of world views" occurs when a psychotherapist sits down with a client or when a shaman meets with a patient, reflects a subtle but crucial factor in the therapeutic encounter. Healer and client both bring to the session a set of assumptions about the nature of the universe, sociocultural mores, the type of information that promotes healing, how it should be applied, and why it works. Cross-cultural observations tell us that the more congruent these assumptions are between healer and healee, the more likely it is that healing will happen.[2] A client who grew up in Japan and believes in the efficacy of acupuncture and yoga, for example, may find her trust undermined by a Western practitioner who displays a cautious or suspicious attitude toward these modalities.

In any curative endeavor, the healer's reactions are pivotal to the therapeutic relationship. If a client reports behavior that violates a shared cultural ethic (many cultures denounce adultery, for example), a response of nonjudgmental acceptance helps combat the demoralization she may feel—and in turn, engenders hope for healing. Even the suggestion that a particular procedure will alleviate distress can optimize the outcome. This happens when, in response to internalizing the healer's belief in the procedure, the sufferer triggers her own innate healing responses.

Although an aura of mystery surrounds the precise catalyst that elicits a healing response in clients, studies suggest that four notable features contribute to productive psychotherapy.[3] More than anything else, an effective therapeutic alliance is characterized by an *emotionally charged and confiding relationship.* The healer cares, and in his caring demonstrates a determination to help the client no matter how dire the circumstances or how dreadful the behavior. This attribute alone is often sufficient cause for improvement in the client's condition. Think of a time, for example, when burdened by a transgression, you dared to confide in a trusted and supportive friend, and were surprised by the relief the confession alone provided.

Second, a therapeutic relationship is enhanced by a *healing setting* that promotes feelings of safety and distinguishes the therapist as a healer. If healing forces are to be mobilized, body and mind must relax and a sense of trust must prevail. The physical tenor of the practitioner's office provides an important backdrop for the needed assurance of confidentiality and support.

Third, an effective alliance rests on a *myth* or a *rationale*—a credible explanation for the symptoms and the prescribed methods for resolving them. The theories of Sigmund Freud form one such rationale; those of B. F. Skinner form another; and the principles of healing by therapeutic touch constitute yet another.

The fourth trademark of an effective healing relationship is the *active participation by client and healer in a ritual or procedure they both believe is therapeutic.* Upon viewing a video on the advantages of relaxation and imagery, for example, a client more inclined to practice the session exercises on her own will reap the benefit of quickened improvement.

Shamanic relationships, too, demonstrate these qualities. The shaman is committed to the welfare of the sufferer and shows compassion for her plight. Using the accoutrements of the profession—drum, rattle, and possibly candles, medicine pouch, and incense—he creates a special setting to enhance the client's sense of comfort and safety. Journeying provides the rationale for the acquisition and application of healing information. Finally, the client participates in the healing by being drawn into an altered state of consciousness or by focusing on her own intent to heal. She may also take part in the ritual, in whatever way the shaman prescribes.

Left to our *own* devices when distressed, we may try various remedies—rest, diversionary activities, exercise, improved nutrition, or attempts at better communication—and we may succeed in easing our torment. Actually, treatments furnished by psychotherapists and other healers have been termed mere "exaggerations" or "extra developments" of mechanisms we would otherwise put into place for ourselves.[4] Be that as it may, individuals who engage the services of a psychotherapist and those who work with a shaman are apt to find common denominators guiding their paths to recovery.

Altered States of Consciousness

Did you ever emerge from a movie theater and feel yourself so transported by the film that you had difficulty orienting to the external world? Did you ever awaken from a dream unable to shake yourself loose from its grip? Each of these states differs from those of ordinary awareness, and is therefore termed an altered state of consciousness (ASC). A straightforward definition of an ASC is, "narrowed focus to the exclusion of everything else"—similar to the condition of an absentminded professor so lost in his experiment that he is oblivious to the comings and goings of people through his laboratory.

While in an ASC, we perceive information coming in through our senses in unique ways, we may respond to emotional arousal differently, and our thought processes may be changed—all of which can reflect alterations in both intensity and quality. Such a state results from any number of factors. Drug intoxication or high fevers may cause a clouding of consciousness and disorientation. Hallucinogenic substances can modify our perception of sensory stimuli, as well as other mental functions. Exposure to pain, caused by anything from physical abuse to an automobile accident, may prompt amnesia (loss of memory) or dissociation (separation of threatening ideas or painful feelings from the rest of the psyche). Religious or mystical immersions also give rise to ASCs, as does the therapeutic application of hypnosis, guided imagery, or biofeedback. More commonly, we *all* experience ASCs in dreams and in the transition period before falling asleep (hypnogogic state) or waking up (hypnopompic state).

Many labels are given to ASCs. Some, such as "meditation" or "alpha induction," describe the means by which a person enters into the state. Others, such as "inebriation" or "relaxation," describe aspects of being in the state. Adding to the confusion is a diverse assortment of identifying terminology such as "trance," "hypnotic susceptibility," "reverie," and "daydream." Michael Harner uses the term "shamanic state of consciousness" to refer not only to the shaman's trance but also to the "learned awarenesses of shamanic methods and assumptions" derived from that state.[5]

Precisely what transpires in the brain as an ASC ensues is still a matter of conjecture, although today's sophisticated technology is soon likely to pave the way to more tangible insights. As of now, some theoreticians view ASCs as a sequence of events occurring along a continuum of increasing depth (approached as one goes more and more deeply into trance) and at times overlapping with each other. Charles Tart, a leading researcher in states of consciousness, sees ASCs instead as discrete phenomena. He describes a discrete altered state of consciousness as a "qualitative alteration in the overall pattern of mental functioning, such that the experiencer feels his consciousness is radically different from the way it functions ordinarily."[6]

Tart likens a discrete altered state of consciousness to a temporary change in a computer program, such that varying the input changes the output. Psychologically speaking, when drugs, trauma to the central nervous system, or sensory deprivation or overload disrupts the baseline state of ordinary consciousness, the mental processes sustaining ordinary consciousness collapse. The mental system then restructures a new pattern for functioning. The nature of this new pattern, influenced by environmental conditions, physiological factors, emotions, and belief systems, constitutes a discrete altered state of consciousness. The return to ordinary consciousness, or deinduction, follows the same process, moving from disruption of the ASC to reconstruction of the baseline state.

While it is true that all altered states reflect a departure from ordinary waking consciousness, we need to remember that each one is characterized by a unique pattern of mental functioning. Meditation, for example, "empties the mind" or fixes the attention on a single focal point, whereas a guided imagery exercise or a shamanic journey engages the mind in a dynamic "picture show."

Characteristics of ASCs

ASCs affect our body functions, our thinking, our emotions, and our perceptions. The most popularized study of physiological changes was conducted by Herbert Benson, a professor of medicine at Harvard University. In a daring move for 1975, Benson took subjects trained in Transcendental Meditation, yoga, autogenic training, progressive relaxation, or hypnosis, and compared the effects of these various ways of inducing altered states. With little variation, he found a general quieting of the nervous system. In contrast to the fight-or-flight response—which in times of overwhelming stress triggers increases in blood pressure, heart rate, respiration, and metabolism—the "relaxation response" he noted produced a decrease in these functions. When we experience stress, whether from a close call on the freeway or from the unrelenting pressures of day-to-day living, adrenal hormones pump into our bloodstream, taking a toll on our well-being. Benson advocated that these stressful effects could be ameliorated by regularly eliciting the relaxation response.[7] Now, more than twenty years after this pioneering study, mainstream medicine is beginning to take note of such preventive therapeutics in an attempt to decrease the incidence of stress-related illnesses.

ASCs also trigger psychological changes, including alterations in concentration, attention, memory, judgment, and emotional expression.[8] Milton Erickson, founder of the leading contemporary approach to hypnosis, described a hypnotic state as one in which the person can "think, act, and behave as adequately as, and often better than, he can in the ordinary state of psychological awareness, quite possibly because of the intensity of his attention to his task and his freedom from distraction."[9] As we have seen, this narrowing of attention is considered a hallmark of the ASC. It isn't only the absentminded professor who loses a sense of connection with the outside world; captured by the spell of a powerful novel or lost in the enthusiasm of creating a work of art, we *all* succumb to the concentrated focus of natural and self-generated ASCs.

In therapeutic situations the confining and turning in of attention facilitates the processing of problems. These attributes also assist the shamanic practitioner as he travels into nonordinary reality in search of healing information. Even the rhythmic beat of the drum will fade as he begins interacting with the spirit beings inhabiting the shamanic cosmos.

Either amnesia (loss of memory) or hypermnesia (extreme degree of recall) can come into play during altered states. In some instances, the content of an ASC, including the details of a shamanic journey, will recede from memory in much the same way that dream experiences do. In others, individuals in an ASC will recount details of events long forgotten. Judgment, too, can be affected. In response to therapeutically induced altered states, clients frequently become more discerning. ASCs induced by alcohol or drugs, on the other hand, can lead to poor decision making.

When we dream at night or daydream during waking hours, we move into a state of consciousness governed by *primary process thinking*—that is, our feelings, thoughts, memories, impressions, and insights become less subject to rational censorship. Primary process thinking, with its lack of regard for reality and logic, can accommodate the coexistence of opposites such as "hot snow" or "a smiling pit bull." Its counterpart, *secondary process thinking*, is based on reason and calls on the more linear processes needed for solving problems and forming opinions and judgments. Success in today's world often hinges on these processes, commonly called "left brain thinking," rather than on the more emotional, intuitive, and creative dynamics attributed to the right side of the brain and primary process thinking, or on shamanic tradition.

Suspecting that secondary process thinking is likely to be diminished in an ASC, some individuals enter into altered states somewhat fearful of losing self-control; others welcome this loss of control. To help overcome fear, therapists working with hypnosis or guided imagery may suggest that clients keep their eyes open, or envision a place of safety. When teaching the journeying technique, therapists inform clients of the role they play in determining the course of events, and of their option to leave the journey at any moment simply by exiting through the "entryway."

The fear of feelings surfacing is well-founded, for emotional changes do accompany ASC experiences. Extremes of emotion can occur, as well as an abrupt emergence of intense feelings. On the other end of the spectrum, some individuals become emotionally detached, viewing the imagery as though it were a movie and describing intense experiences with no affect.

More surprising, perhaps, are the perceptual changes associated with ASCs. Distortions in body image may occur: a person may experience a portion of her body as very large or small, heavy or weightless. Numbness, tingling, and analgesia are also common. A sense of depersonalization (feeling detached from oneself) or of merging with others or the world may arise as well. How an individual regards these distortions often depends on their context: in a delirious drug-induced state they may be frightening, whereas in a spiritual setting they may appear as "transcendent," much like the shaman's experience of merging with his power animal.

Other perceptual changes include hallucinations (seeing, hearing, smelling, tasting, or touching something not physically present), illusions (misinterpretations of sensory stimuli), and synesthesias (experiencing sounds as colors, or sights as tastes, caused by stimulation of one sense organ producing sensations in another). Placing heightened emphasis on these ASC perceptions may be revelatory for a person seeking insight or for a shaman in search of a cure. But subjectivity of this sort spouted by an intoxicated individual might only turn off the audience he has invariably cornered.

During an ASC, time is experienced differently, as well. At the end of the experience, a person who has been in "trance time," as it is called, may have no idea how much time has elapsed. For some individuals, time accelerates; for others, it slows down; still others report a feeling of timelessness.

A psychotherapeutic session itself may prompt an ASC. The narrowing of attention on a problematic issue can be so intense that the feelings bubbling up may crowd out all other awarenesses. At the end of such sessions, clients have been known to remark, "It seems like only ten minutes have gone by" or "I feel like I've been in a trance."

Upon emerging from an ASC, most people have difficulty articulating the nature of their experience. All the same, they are likely to associate it with feelings of renewal, rejuvenation, or rebirth. The ecstatic writings of mystics overflow with this sense of new hope. Other outcomes are also possible, however, as we will see in the following section.

Adaptive and Maladaptive ASCs

ASCs can be of profound benefit to our mental health, yet they can also spawn disjointed experiences and disruptive consequences.[10] There is a vast difference between the contented absorption in nature engendered by a wilderness hike, for instance, and the terrifying assault of a drug-induced hallucination. A wise approach to our own states of consciousness entails an understanding of the distinctions between adaptive and maladaptive ASCs.

Adaptive ASCs stimulate a healthy self-awareness. Primary process thinking alone can put us in touch with vital and creative parts of ourselves. Some years ago a client told me that although he was taking vocal lessons and was committed to improving his voice, he could feel within himself a block against "really belting out a song." He wondered if some early event was responsible for the block. We went on to talk about his childhood and the influences that shaped his love for music—a passion neither understood nor supported by his hard-working parents. Then, positioned comfortably in a reclining chair, with the room slightly darkened, he responded to my suggestions for releasing tension and gradually moved into a state of relaxation. While in this ASC, he began to describe several attempts to practice singing in his childhood bedroom. Suddenly overcome by emotion, he recalled a time when his mother pounded on the door and told him to stop because, as she put it, "boys don't sing—they play baseball." The awakening of this memory catalyzed not only a release of feelings about the painful rebuff but also an awareness that he was carrying a false voice of authority in his head. Dealing with this voice took his psychological work to another level, which helped him move past the block and begin singing with gusto.

Psychiatrist A. M. Ludwig says of such an experience, "In some instances the psychological regression found in ASC will . . . enable man to transcend the bounds of logic and formality or express repressed needs and desires in a socially sanctioned and constructive way."[11] The ASC-induced reexperiencing of the painful childhood event described above led to a beneficial resolution of a painful dilemma. If left untended, this man's despair may have sabotaged his commitment to singing, or may have increased his stress levels to the point of generating physical illness. Discovering new knowledge, garnering experience, or finding inspiration through an ASC can all help ameliorate emotional conflicts and amplify creativity.

ASCs in group settings can be equally adaptive. One of the most famous examples of an *en masse* ASC took place at Woodstock in August 1969. Drugs aside, music transported participants into a realm of hope for a more love-filled world. Group ASCs, large or small, bring about a sense of identification, purpose, or cohesion, all the while reducing the fears and tensions so often present in collective efforts. Strangers at the outset of an intensely focused weekend retreat who are furthered in their efforts through guided

ASC experiences often end up relating to one another with enthusiasm and support. Likewise, the shaman's drumming at a healing ritual will transport attendees into a trance state, bonding them in their shared hope for the patient's recovery.

Maladaptive ASCs tap into a more dysfunctional side of human nature. A person with or without the assistance of alcohol or drugs may move into an altered state to escape from responsibilities, tensions, or other discomforts. Faced with an emotional threat in this state, he may resort to dissociation or depersonalization to prevent undesirable feelings from invading the rest of his psyche. Walter Mitty-type daydreaming, if taken to the extreme of feeling out of touch with oneself, reaches a depersonalizing tilt. Estrangement from the core self also occurs with dissociation, which shifts an individual into the persona of another self—the hallmark of a multiple personality disorder. (Although depersonalization and dissociation are maladaptive in these instances, they are important adaptive mechanisms when physical or psychological survival is at stake; indeed, they can serve as lifelines to a child exposed to repeated abuse.)

The breakthrough, or near-breakthrough, of forbidden unconscious impulses during an ASC may lead to psychotic episodes or panic attacks. A person with manic-depressive illness may, in an extreme manic state, become so overtaken by beliefs and feelings incongruent with external reality and so driven by primal energy that he will go on a spree—taking trips to exotic places, having sexual encounters with strangers, or wantonly spending money on himself and others, all with no regard for the social or financial destruction left in his wake. Panic attacks are another concern, leaving an individual unable to pinpoint the source of impending doom that overwhelms him, and hence causing him to live in an ongoing altered state of dread and fear.

The emergence of unconscious conflicts may also be acted out in insidious rituals of possession, witchcraft, or other power-laden altered-state ordeals; in life, as in fairy tales, such activities hint at evildoings and can elicit a sense of foreboding. Neurological disturbances sometimes occur during ASCs, including the strange sensory and perceptual distortions of the prodromal stage of migraine headaches. Trances induced by highway driving, assembly-line work, or other activities involving prolonged exposure to repeated stimuli engender boredom and can lead to faulty judgment, sleepiness, or an increased risk of accident.

One of the most celebrated aspects of maladaptive ASCs is suggestibility. The belief that a hypnotist can command a subject to engage in foolish behavior was a popular theme in television comedies and nightclub acts of the 1950s. Still in vogue are film clips showing Hitler's protestations of racial supremacy to mesmerized audiences. It is easy to see how a narrowed focus of attention can prostrate itself to a commanding presence, causing harm to the individual, if not to society.

Recognition of the adaptive and maladaptive potentials of ASCs is essential to anyone wishing to utilize this healing modality in a responsible way. The burden of discernment rests with both the practitioner who takes on the role of navigator and the individual who sets out to raise her awareness through these states. Inherent in the ethics of utilizing ASCs is an understanding of the power of suggestibility, and here the onus rests with the therapist to employ altered states *solely in pursuit of the client's psychological integrity.* The therapist must secure adequate training, must properly educate the client in the technique, must honor guidelines governing appropriate touch in therapeutic relationships, and must avail himself of consultation should difficulties arise. The client's responsibility is to inquire into the therapist's background and orientation, and to question the slightest indication of ethical violation.

Imagery

Imagination is a universal experience. Even people who say they have no imagination, or an inability to image objects, engage in imaging without realizing it. They do this each time they have an *internal perception of a sound, sight, smell, taste, touch, or movement that produces a mental likeness of the original stimulus.* In mentioning a familiar building, describing a scrumptious meal, or humming a favorite melody, we are mentally calling up something that at the moment is not available through one of our senses.

This *internal perception* is considered psychologically and physiologically equivalent to an *external perception*, so much so that the person imaging an event may respond as though the event were actually happening. For example, hearing an account of a friend's trip to the dentist—replete with details of the facial masks, suction machine, overhead light, and hand-held drill—can trigger anxiety, as if we ourselves were seated in the dental chair.

Imagery is inextricably linked to altered states. In fact, images propel one's movement into nonordinary reality and actuate the experiences occurring within it. The shaman, in response to the beating drum, visualizes the terrain from which he will ascend, descend, or project his soul through the middle world. The therapist uses images to guide her client into an ASC. But whereas the shaman's imagery of departure is fixed, having been dictated by tradition, the therapist will call upon any number of images, depending on the theoretical model she employs.

Imagery has been central to the work of indigenous shamans. The shaman today, like his ancestors, is able to "see" an invasion of foreign energy encased in his patient's body, "hear" the call of a lost soul, and "feel" the brush of his power animal against his leg. Imagery as a psychological tool, however, is a relatively recent addition.

Historical Considerations

Shamanism, along with mythology, mysticism, and magic, contributed to the use of imagery in the Western world. Certainly, it influenced the practices of temple priests in ancient Egypt and Greece who evoked and interpreted dreams for healing purposes. In Greece and its surrounding territories, the cult of Asclepius—god of healing—built scores of temples as healing centers. Here patients fasted, wore special robes, slept in sanctuaries, and were told to note whatever images arose during the hypnogogic state immediately prior to sleep, particularly those in which Asclepius appeared. The images were then used to diagnose and treat the patients' illnesses.[12]

Hippocrates was trained in Asclepian methods, and subsequent generations of physicians incorporated the power of imagination into their healing practices. These endeavors came to a halt, however, in the Middle Ages, when throughout Europe and the British Isles, the use of imagery thrived only in other sectors of society. Folk medicine circles were dominated by female practitioners who aligned with the forces of nature in shamanic-like ways. Processions, shrines, and relics sanctioned by the Catholic Church triggered images of cures and miracle healings. In England the Church also supported the use of "incubation sleep"—similar to Ascelpius' application of hypnogogic imagery—as inspired by two martyrs, Saints Cosmos and Damian.[13]

Even though Descartes's mind-and-body split of the seventeenth century left little to the "imagination," by the late nineteenth century in both Europe and the United States, imagery had become a topic of investigation in the burgeoning field of psychology. Freud would press his hand against the foreheads of patients, telling them to note the images that emerged. It is said that he was so disturbed by these images that he eventually abandoned the approach.[14] Whether or not this story is true, his shift of focus to more verbal forms of psychoanalysis, along with the growing popularity of behaviorism, led to a decline in the use of imagery in the United States during the first half of the twentieth century. In Europe, however, many practitioners continued to explore imagery, devising various methods of treatment that expanded the repertoire of Western healing practices.

By the 1970s gestalt, cognitive, and even behavior modification therapists in the United States had reintroduced the use of imagery. Enriched by such innovators as Jerome Singer and Joseph Shorr, and influenced by Milton Erickson's rejuvenation of hypnosis, imagery-based psychotherapies soon began to flourish. This rekindling of interest coincided with a renaissance of imagery in the treatment of *physical* disease. In the late 1970s Carl Simonton, Stephanie Matthews-Simonton, and James Creighton brought the topic to center stage by publishing a book on overcoming cancer by stimulating the immune system through the use of healing imagery.[15] Jeanne Achterberg's 1985 book *Imagery in Healing*, with its revealing subtitle, *Shamanism and Modern Medicine*, formally placed shamanic approaches side by side with established healing practices. "Shamanism *is* the medicine of the imagination," she states, and then goes on to describe the many ways in which contemporary medicine and the behavioral and social sciences incorporate the use of imagery.[16]

Dr. Achterberg describes the client as an active participant and the "shaman/scientist" as a teacher. The shaman/scientist instructs the client in aspects of the disease process; counsels her in the use of various treatment modalities; teaches her how to move into an ASC; and guides her in the use of images relevant to her diagnosis, treatment, and personal defenses. In this way the shaman/scientist serves to activate the "natural, but often latent human ability" to employ imagery in the healing of physical affliction.[17]

Imagery, as Hippocrates' forebears knew, triggers physiological responses. Today we know that it does so because it engages the same neural pathways and networks in the brain as actual perception. Envisioning a lemon produces salivation, and images of arousal increase the heart rate. Investigators have found that subjects introduced to specific images will show decreased gastrointestinal activity, increased blood sugar levels, and changes in skin temperature and size of the pupils. The use of biofeedback to treat high blood pressure and migraine headaches is one of many applications that currently capitalize on this body-mind relationship.[18] Moreover, researchers studying the effects of imaging techniques on the immune system have found that they enhance the activity of white blood cells and the efficiency of hormonal responses.[19]

The effects of imagery on the body carry tremendous implications for health-care professionals. Andrew Weil, who practices natural and preventive medicine, tells us that DNA, "the macromolecule that defines life," has within it a natural tendency to trigger spontaneous healing.[20] A vital means for mobilizing this tendency is imagery, he tells us, emphasizing that it is most beneficial when it evokes emotion, as opposed to static, neutral mental pictures. In other words, passion energizes the image into healing action. "Whether the emotion felt is positive or negative seems not to matter; rather it is the intensity of the feeling that gives it power to affect body function," says Weil.[21] A cancer patient with a compelling need for order and cleanliness may effectively visualize the rhythmic strokes of a broom sweeping away the invasive cells. Another cancer patient may have more success envisioning a laser gun bombarding the cells.

Behaviorists, too, furthered the status of imagery by introducing *systematic desensitization*, a technique that while yielding quantifiable results, relies on the imaging of anxiety-arousing situations to reduce anxiety. After constructing a hierarchy of anxiety-producing situations associated with a specific fear, such as fear of riding in elevators, a client envisions the situation of least anxiety while engaging in a deep muscle relaxation procedure. When sufficiently relaxed, he progresses to the next rung on the hierarchical ladder. Continuing in this manner, he eventually reaches the top rung of fear, at which point he images an actual elevator ride. Because the relaxation procedure serves to inhibit fear, the client becomes progressively desensitized to riding in elevators.

This technique bears some resemblance to the recently introduced method of *Eye Movement Desensitization and Reprocessing (EMDR)*, mentioned in chapter 1. A client using EMDR engages in prescribed eye movements while holding in his mind an image of trauma, along with a negative belief about himself. This method is said to change the way the brain processes information about painful events, resulting in diminished anxiety. Effectiveness of the procedure is assessed through rating scales.[22]

Today we know a lot about imagery, so much so that its use is firmly entrenched in the psychotherapist's armamentarium of techniques. All branches of psychology utilize imagery in one form or another, from the rehearsal of upcoming challenges to the psychodynamic recall of childhood conflicts. A visit to the therapist's office, however, is not necessary to benefit from ASC imagery. As individuals going about our daily business, we routinely engage in imaginal activities. We call upon daydreams, guided meditations, and other configurations of imagery in our attempts to relieve overwhelming stresses, give meaning to our lives, and awaken hope for the future.

Psychological Applications of Imagery

Compared with the internal perceptions we access in our everyday waking state, the imagery we experience in an ASC is more intense. As we have seen, these spontaneous images tend to be less subject to reason and censorship, and their organization appears simpler, more primitive, and more indicative of primary process thinking. It is also true that calling forth *specific* images to foster behavioral change or promote healing can activate mechanisms associated with *secondary process* thinking.

Here is how this phenomenon occurs. Putting the imagination to work produces not only physiological effects but feeling states as well, as discussed earlier. Imagining a dreaded confrontation with an adversary, for example, will give rise to a feeling of *anxiety* in addition to a pounding heart, rapid breathing, and other physical symptoms. It is possible to reverse these consequences by constructing images involving reasoned dialogue and appropriate assertions. In other words, effectively imaging an interaction that leads to negotiation can lower anxiety levels while relaxing the body.

Empirical studies indicate that "imagery rehearsal" of this sort does influence behavior, suggesting that mental imaging can impact on real-life situations. Such effects have been noted in the sphere of physical performance, where research reveals that mental practice as an adjunct to physical practice can enhance athletic skills.[23, 24] One study shows that during a period of no physical practice, novice skiers who mentally rehearsed a skiing procedure later outperformed those who did not.[25]

Imaginal activity improves psychological performance as well. A study group of burn patients who participated in relaxation and imagery exercises prior to having their wounds treated felt less anxiety and pain than those who did not.[26] Students with text anxiety have found that guided imagery not only reduces their levels of worry but also increases their academic performance.[27] The use of directed visual imagery (involving the introduction of specific images) has diminished the degree of depression in psychiatric patients[28] and improved the cognitive functioning of nursing home residents.[29]

The application of imagery in psychotherapy occurs in both subtle and obvious ways. Imagery is used to generate information, identify and work through problems, promote empathic understanding, and change attitudes and feelings. Sometimes outcomes arise naturally in the unfolding of a session as productive images surface in the therapeutic dialogue. Other times, specific techniques are utilized to target images, cultivate their meanings, and harvest their clues. The workings of these more obvious approaches to imagery are illustrated in the following four examples.

Carl Jung's technique of *active imagination* shows how information emerges through the application of imagery.[30] Based on the belief that contents of the unconscious appear in conscious form as images, active imagination invites the individual to focus on a memorable yet incomprehensible dream or visual image she has experienced. In a daydreamlike state she begins interacting with the image through drawing, writing, or movement. The ensuing motif gives expression to her underlying tensions and simultaneously provides the therapist with an informational road map to use in directing the therapeutic work.

Guided affective imagery (GAI), introduced by German psychiatrist Hanscarl Leuner, targets specific problems and sets the stage for working through them. Here the therapist presents the client with ten prescribed situations, including one that has to do with a house (symbolic of the self) and another that entails climbing a mountain (symbolic of aspiration and motivation). Leuner explains, "[Imaging] evokes intense latent feelings that are relevant to the patient's problems. Techniques for the guiding and transformation of imagery lead to desirable changes in both affect and attitudes toward life situations."[31]

As the therapist listens to descriptions of the client's imagery, often florid with feeling, he comes to understand what the client has been unable to identify through verbal explorations. If a man attempting to reach the top of the imaginary mountain cries when he encounters his dead father on the trail, the therapist's empathic perception of the client's situation will be enhanced. By the same token, when the imaging client experiences someone else's reality in such scenarios, his understanding of others may deepen.

The transformation of images during such exercises can be profound. I once asked a client struggling with protracted grief over the death of a friend to image her sadness. Initially, she envisioned a stone so hard that it was resistant to the forces of nature attempting to penetrate its surface. She felt a part of herself inside the stone, compressed by its mass, struggling to be free. As she puzzled over what might soften the mass, she saw the rock turn into a ball of dough, elastic and responsive to her touch. In subsequent weeks, her grief slowly loosened, giving way to a flexibility that allowed for ceremonies of closure and farewell.

The use of imagery in the *crystal ball technique* can help change attitudes as well. In this case, the therapist asks the client to image a crystal ball and to see inside it a future time in which the problem she is grappling with is effectively solved. The client, in creating this imaginary future, not only entertains the notion of a resolution but also opens to the need for taking steps to *reach* this goal. Previously convinced that nothing could alter her situation, she uncovers an attitude of possibility.

Psychosynthesis, which strives to harmonize components of the unconscious with the rest of the personality, also relies on imagery. In the following case example, imaging both provides a diagnosis and presents a solution:

> One patient described her problem in the first session as having a dominating husband. She was asked to visualize the way she felt about the relationship and saw herself as a little bird being tightly held in a clenched hand. The bird was frightened, helpless, and could not get away. It was then suggested that she imagine the hand opening, and she saw the bird fly away to a nearby branch. She was surprised to note, however, that the bird would not venture far from the hand and that it was a "sugar bird" that fed on sugar provided by humans, having forgotten how to get food for itself in the natural way and thus having to depend upon people to

live. The patient was able to see through this visualization that she had allowed her husband to dominate her because she felt more secure being taken care of like a child. At this point she was asked to try to see the bird eating the kind of food that wild birds normally eat. She felt that the bird would have to move to another island where there was more vegetation and imagined [it] riding [on] a fishing boat since the other island was too far away to fly [to]. The bird was happy that there were plenty of seeds to eat there and that he could also enjoy eating sugar from time to time for a treat. This session alone led to a marked improvement in the patient's relationship to her husband who was delighted, as it turned out, to have her assume more responsibility and independence and did not try to "crush" her as she had feared.[32]

This description illustrates several characteristics of the imaging process. When the client was asked to visually represent her dilemma, the resulting image—displaying her feelings of being trapped, helpless, and powerless—was both immediate and symbolic. Her construction of a suitable site in which the bird could eat natural food reflects the ability of imagery to recast a scenario in advantageous terms.

This account also demonstrates one of the most therapeutic attributes of the imagery process—the circumvention of defenses through content veiled in metaphor. Because imagery scenes originate from within, clients can usually grasp their implications. Interpretations offered by the therapist, on the other hand, require a response from the conscious mind, with all its attendant defenses. Had the therapist in this case example interpreted the woman's relationship with her husband, she may have spent time discussing, if not contesting, the accuracy of his observations. More importantly, she would not have had the satisfaction of working with self-generated information.

In my experience, when the imagery process is approached by a therapist capable of ensuring an atmosphere of safety, the client's defenses remain intact—that is, her unconscious does not blast forth with images that overwhelm the defense system. The unconscious, in such instances, tends to present material that the client's conscious self is capable of considering. When the content that arises suggests weighty and unacknowledged emotion for which the client is unprepared, as often occurs in dreams, she may ignore the images or casually dismiss them as irrelevant.

In a safe environment, in other words, the healing action of imagery does not incapacitate the defenses; nor does it require the client to achieve insight. During Ericksonian hypnosis, the therapist may tell a story to a client in an ASC. Interwoven throughout the story, which metaphorically recapitulates the client's dilemma, are options that may serve as alternate ways of viewing the problem. Without commentary or interpretation, the therapist allows the experience to continue its effects in the client's unconscious after she leaves the session. She may begin the following session by reporting on a shift in perspective. Or later in the session she may casually describe the remarkable discovery of a new idea—one curiously different from any of the options presented in the story. The point is that the unconscious will respond to the *possibility* of change, often by creating its own response to a quandary.

The scientist/shaman concept outlined by Dr. Achterberg extends into the psychotherapeutic arena. Just as patients suffering from physical illness are taught to use mental pictures to strengthen the immune system, so can clients grappling with psychological distress be taught to activate healing images to promote mental and emotional well-being. While it is true that the focused attention of therapist and client can result in a spontaneous trance state and in the intuitive recovery of healing images and ideas, the psychotherapist can also teach the principles of ASC imagery. Enlisting an individual's active participation in her healing both demystifies the psychotherapeutic process and empowers her.

Shamanic Imagery

The vividness and vitality of shamanic imagery, which for millennia illumined the shamans' journeys, are now experienced by more and more people outside indigenous cultures. One reason for this increased exposure may be that Michael Harner, in his book *The Way of the Shaman*, has provided instructions for individuals interested in journeying; and since its publication in 1980, it has attracted a wide and enthusiastic readership.

The imagery encountered on an initial journey is often as lucid as that experienced on subsequent ones. Here, for example, is a classic description of a client's first journey into the lower world:

Mary reclines in a comfortable chair. Over her ears is a set of head-phones attached by a cord to a Walkman that rests in her lap. She starts the cassette, and as the drum begins its resonating beat, she envisions herself in the mountains next to a cave—a favorite hik-ing destination. She feels herself on all fours, crawling into the cave. At first, the darkness overtakes her, but as she moves for-ward, she catches a glimmer of light. Slowly inching toward it, she savors the cool, moist air on her skin and smells the mustiness of the damp walls. Reaching the exit, she sees a sun-filled meadow stretched out before her. Scrambling to her feet, she delights in this lower world panorama—the lush grass, the tall trees skirting three sides of the meadow, and a river rippling westward.

"I'm putting out a call for my power animal," she says timidly. Birds are flying overhead, but she sees no sign of an animal in the meadow or between the trees. After repeating her call more stri-dently, she notices a fox ambling by, but it pays her no heed. Then she hears the cry of a raven, and wonders if her power animal is to be a bird.

Walking toward the river, she speculates on the possibility of her power coming through a creature of the water. She sits on the river-bank and once again repeats her request for an animal. This time a deer emerges from the trees. She waits until it reaches the water and lowers its head for a drink. Then as it turns toward her, she asks, "Are you my power animal?" The deer, moving closer, looks into Mary's eyes, whereupon a shiver of excitement passes through her. Without hearing an answer, she knows the deer is her ally.

The deer begins to walk away from the river, at which point it becomes clear that Mary is to follow. The rhythm of the walking, woman following deer, strangely matches the cadence of the drum. They walk for a long time, only to arrive at the edge of the meadow where Mary first emerged into this world. Hearing the drumbeat quicken, she knows the journey is about to end. She thanks the deer for coming to be with her and tells him she looks forward to visiting him again. Then she enters the cave and works her way back to ordinary reality.[33]

For many journeyers, imagery is the most pronounced feature of their sojourns in the spirit world. Seeing and hearing a flowing river, feeling the gaze of the power animal, moving in rhythm with the creature—all these sensory experiences contribute to the connection forged between the journeyer and the shamanic world. First-time journeyers frequently report that this world sparks feelings of connection, protection, and safety. They quickly pick up on the nonverbal cues of the power animal and on the information relayed through its activity, much as a newborn recognizes the cues emanating from the loved ones in his surroundings.

The Role of the Unconscious

Where does this journeying activity take place? Does the soul of the shaman move out of his body into another realm or are his travels confined to the mental domain of the imagination? The shaman would say that his soul visits other dimensions of reality. Most psychologists would not doubt that shamans display a remarkable facility for imaging realms far beyond the ordinary, but would be reluctant to classify these realms as "other worlds."

The riddle of the shaman is best solved by probing the role of the unconscious. Anyone influenced by a psychodynamic or Jungian orientation will concede that the unconscious has a pervasive and consequential, yet mysterious influence on human behavior. No corner of activity escapes its canvas, which absorbs personal as well as transpersonal impressions.

The *personal unconscious* is Jung's term for the region in each individual's psyche that contains elements of her experiences, including those she has forgotten or repressed.[34] Jung also proposed the existence of a *collective unconscious,* a region of the psyche common to all humankind. The collective unconscious, unlike the personal unconscious, is inherited and carries memory traces from the ancestral past, including vestiges of prehuman, or animal, experience. Jung said:

> The instinctive, archaic basis of the mind is a matter of plain objec-
> tive fact and is no more dependent upon individual experience or
> personal choice than is the inherited structure and functioning of
> the brain or any other organ. Just as the body has its evolutionary
> history and shows clear traces of the various evolutionary stages,
> so too does the psyche.[35]

The collective unconscious is composed of instincts and archetypes. *Instincts* are basic drives—inherited tendencies such as the
proclivity to seek out food or the urge for self-assertion. These drives, which are exhibited by every member of the species, manifest
as *archetypes*, symbolic images that take the form of a theme, or
motif, held in the collective unconscious and activated into representation by life situations.[36] There exists, for example, a generic
mother motif built into the human brain as a result of generations
of exposure to mother figures. Consequently, a baby is born with a
preformed unconscious conception of a generic mother that influences how he will experience his actual mother. The baby's mother, in effect, takes on the overlay of the projected archetype.

Most psychotherapists accept the notion of the personal
unconscious, and view this region of the psyche as the source of
unfamiliar images triggered in ASCs. Many, however, do not consider the possibility of the collective unconscious. Indeed, they
would look askance at anyone who suggests that an image may
represent an "archetype derived from the accumulated experiences of humankind." And yet when a shaman journeys into
other realms and encounters animal and spirit beings, ancient
themes of being and healing seem to be activated.

Early in the history of the species, human life was dependent on
the powers of nature, and on attuning to her forces and rhythms.
Ways of the animals, subtleties of the weather, the whereabouts of
food supplies, and many other aspects of the natural environment
occupied the attention of our early forebears. Learning of nature's

medicinal offerings, they devised methods for healing wounds and illnesses. Over the millennia, the psyche became imprinted with all these motifs of plant life, animal lore, and the many means of surviving in the wild.

Jung went so far as to assume that by peeling away the collective unconscious layer by layer, we would eventually come upon the psychology of the amoeba. His belief was that patternings from the animal and even plant kingdoms are etched into the human psyche, that forces and beings experienced by earlier inhabitants of the planet, though imperceptible to us today, have left their imprint on us.[37]

This notion of a collective sharing is akin to the holistic concept that all of life is connected. The subjective experience of moving into a dimension of consciousness outside of the personal self—of the soul traveling along a web of interconnectedness to parallel realities—is within the bounds of the feasible, according to transpersonal psychologists, Jungian theoreticians, and generations of mystics.

A fluid relationship between the conscious and the unconscious is central to psychological health. Traumatic memories and unacceptable impulses housed in the unconscious drain psychic energy from the body and mind. Held back by defense mechanisms such as denial and repression, the forbidden contents wait for a lowering of the threshold between the conscious and the unconscious, then spill over into everyday awareness, provoking anxiety and fear, or panic, terror, or extreme depression. But just as the unconscious is the repository for repressed material, so too is it the receptacle for healing forces. For this reason, individuals who through short-term crisis intervention, through long-term in-depth therapy, or on their own are able to tap into these forces, will emerge from such a crisis enriched by new knowledge and strength. Revitalized, they will demonstrate a higher level of functioning and a greater degree of emotional stability.

Shamanic initiates undergo a similar process, as described in chapter 1. The exodus from this trial, too, is marked by greater psychological integrity. A shamanic candidate, like an individual grappling with emotional dilemmas, is forced to interact with eruptions from the unconscious, and thereby bring them to consciousness. In each instance of healing and strengthening, vital instincts are retrieved and archetypal themes are activated.

All of us, whether healers, seekers, or both, share a common denominator. Like the fruit of the apple and the orange, we are meant to mature into our potential and have at our disposal natural resources to further that evolution. As the rain, sun, and soil nourish the fruit trees, healing environments, altered states of consciousness, imagery, and dynamics of the unconscious catalyze our growth.

How the Cradle Is Rocked

The shaman and the psychologist, resting under the tree, are lost in conscious reverie. The shaman thinks back on his ancestors and all that brought him to his calling. He remembers watching his grandmother evoke the spirits when people came for healing. He wonders why the world knows so little about this custom. The psychologist ponders the direction of her work, thinking back to earlier years when, lost in books, she felt the promise of humanity's redemption. Puzzled now by a pull between the opposing forces of scientism and humanism, she hopes to find a middle ground.

WOODEN ROCKING CRADLES WERE HOUSEHOLD FIXTURES A CENTURY ago. Now we have bassinets on wheels, infant bouncers, jump seats, and wind-up swings. No matter what the device may be, the message is, baby likes movement. For many infants in this world, however, the way their cradles are rocked does not resonate with the inner rhythm of their beings; something is askew in their relationships with their caregivers. All about us are children whose well-being is compromised by a lack of loving attention, as well as psychologically wounded adults who act out their pain by harming others or themselves.

At the turn of the last century, moms and dads had no manuals and no TV documentaries to turn to for instruction; most of them parented in much the same way they were parented, rocking their babies' cradles the way theirs were rocked. Then psychology began to offer information on human development and motivation. Freud's early contributions emphasized the pleasure-seeking behaviors of the libido (the sexual energy arising from biological drives of the id), viewing infant behavior as propelled by instinctual impulses. More recent evidence suggests that libidinal energy is actually *people* seeking.[1] In order to physically and psychologically survive and mature, an infant needs people to care for him. The first developmental task in life—bonding with caretakers—serves this purpose. Togetherness, we are learning, motivates large chunks of behavior from the first breath of life to the last. This need for connectedness, for loving acceptance and shared experience with other human beings, is familiar to us all.

Not as readily understood is the need for separation. After bonding with his parent, the vulnerable and dependent infant develops mobility and, in the process, is propelled toward autonomy—which helps shape his individuality. The word *no* becomes a favorite refrain, announcing a stage many parents would rather skip. In this movement toward autonomy, the conflict between connection and separation makes its obvious debut. It begins, however, the day we are born. And our experience of these opposing demands establishes a pattern for life.

Attachment

An infant's unfolding relationship with his caregivers begins even before birth. Pregnancy is riddled with questions: Who is this baby? What sort of personality does he have? What will he be like in one year? In twenty?

Let's take a look at Nick, an infant who has just experienced an uncomplicated natural childbirth. Emerging from the birth canal, he is wide-eyed and alert, gazing directly at his father, who having assisted in the delivery, lifts him up and places him in his mother's arms. Something miraculous permeates the air as mother and father expand their connectedness through the new life in their midst. In the following weeks this yearned for child receives an abundance of undivided attention and delighted adulation from parents well prepared for his arrival. Nick is off to a good start, for his task of bonding is anchored in loving responsiveness from his parents.

Regrettably, Nick's story may be more an exception than the rule, situated as it is at the more promising end of a continuum that ranges from optimally supportive and nourishing to marginally attentive and outright abusive. What happens within infants who have tenuous bonds with their caretakers, and whose prospects for an emotionally secure future are less promising? Although the bonding between a baby and his caretakers appears as natural and spontaneous as a rose blooming on a bush, providing an environment conducive to blossoming involves subtleties we have known little about.

Environmental Influences

Nick's initial gaze at his father shows a capacity parents never thought existed years ago: newborns are keenly responsive to their environments. Not only do two-day-old infants show spontaneous expressions of interest, surprise, happiness, distress, or disgust,[2] they will actually imitate a smile, an expression of sadness, or a look of surprise appearing on the face of an adult nearby.[3] What's more, newborns are far brighter than we suspected. In a study of three-week-old infants researchers gave them one of two differently shaped pacifiers to suck, later placing them side by side in front of the babies and watching their reactions. The infants spent more time looking at those they had just sucked.[4] They were able to visually recognize an object they had experienced only through touch—a remarkable feat, given that the mental functioning of three week olds is usually considered too undifferentiated to help them identify anything!

What, then, is the experience of sensitive and discerning babies who encounter adverse conditions very early in life? For decades such ponderings have occupied the attention of developmental specialists, many of whom have spent hours studying infants in a vast array of settings. In the 1940s psychoanalyst René Spitz observed how infants fare when separated from their mothers. Infants confined to a hospital for several months, he found, succumbed to a type of depression characterized by sadness, apathy, and withdrawal. When reunited with their mothers, only some of them recovered. Spitz concluded that children who are separated from their mothers during the first year of life are subject to potentially irreversible physical regressions and psychological disorders.[5]

About the same time, psychoanalyst John Bowlby also focused on maternal deprivation, eventually coining the term "attachment" to describe the infant-caretaker bond. Bowlby publicized the work of a colleague named James Robertson, who after studying infants in institutions, defined three phases of disengagement for babies separated from their caregivers: *protest* (crying, clinging, and screaming after the parents' departure), followed by *despair* (listlessness and disinterest in surroundings and food), and finally *detachment* (lack of recognition of mother when she visited and lack of crying when she left).[6] In a report on maternal deprivation presented to the World Health Organization in the early 1950s, Bowlby consolidated study outcomes from a number of researchers. A markedly consistent pattern emerged: school-age children who had been separated from their mothers in infancy exhibited superficial relationships, emotional impoverishment, lack of empathy for others, deceit, thievery, and an inability to concentrate.[7]

This pattern of early deprivation negatively affecting later behavior has stood the test of time. Psychologist Mary Ainsworth in the 1960s and 1970s conducted cross-cultural home studies of infant-mother relationships.[8, 9] The similarities in her findings led her to classify attachment behaviors on the basis of an infant's use of adults as "secure bases," reactions to strangers, and responses to separation and reunion.[10] She then devised an assessment procedure capable of determining an infant's security of attachment to parent figures. This procedure was a boon to the research world, paving the way to longitudinal studies that compared infant attachment with later psychological adjustment.[11]

Psychologists Alan Sroufe and Byron Egeland made use of Ainsworth's assessment tool in 1974, when they embarked on a twenty-year study of infants from low-income families. They found that as the children approached school age, those who had been securely attached in infancy showed the most ego resiliency, self-esteem, independence, and capacity for positive interaction with other children.[12] Psychologist Robert Karen, who had access to Sroufe's unpublished reports, points out that when the same children were reevaluated in their early teenage years, those with a history of secure attachment maintained relationship advantages over those less securely attached.[13]

As any student of Psychology 101 knows, even animals have been included in the study of attachment behaviors. In the 1960s Harry Harlow and his colleagues at the University of Wisconsin studied the effects of inanimate surrogate mothers on baby monkeys. The monkeys were raised with a soft "terry-cloth mother" and a "wire mother" made of hard mesh material, each of which was furnished with a bottle for feeding. Consistently, the young monkeys preferred the cloth mothers, no matter which surrogate provided the food.[14] Another group of monkeys, raised in isolation, began acting much like human schizophrenics, mutely staring into space, exhibiting rocking and other repetitive behaviors, and engaging in self-injurious activities.[15]

Thus, behavioral research provides weighty support for the importance of early mother-child relationships* and of contact comfort in the development of emotional responses. Interestingly, the results of these studies have catapulted research into a new dimension now that brain development and functioning have become factored into the bonding equation.

Seeing photographs of infants' brains is almost commonplace today as we thumb through weekly news publications or tune into

---

* Although original research targeted infants with their mothers in the nurturing role, in recent years fathers and other caregivers have been providing attending and nurturing sustenance.

the broadcast media. In a 1997 issue of *Newsweek* devoted to infants and children, positron-emission tomography (PET) shows the brain of an orphan institutionalized shortly after birth with scant activity in the temporal lobes (the region that receives information from the senses and regulates emotions). The article states that children who have been physically abused early in life are especially at risk for compromised brain function. Due to "hair-trigger" alertness and ongoing fear and trauma, a continuing release of stress hormones overrides the processing of natural emotional experiences. Evidence indicates that in these children, the brain regions responsible for emotion are 20 to 30 percent smaller than in normal children.[16]

By contrast, based on data from a variety of disciplines, including neurobiology, evolutionary biology, developmental psychology, and neurochemistry, researcher Allan Schore explains that attachment behaviors have an imprinting effect on a baby's developing nervous system. He concludes that when a mother attunes to her baby—engaging in eye contact while signaling delight and approval in the infant's beingness and behavior—she is stimulating "reward centers" in the brain that facilitate the growth of neural pathways.[17]

This is a far cry from the approach to infant and child care advocated earlier in the century when libidinal energy was viewed as sexual and the recommended parenting style was nontactile and emotionally aloof. In the 1920s, for example, prominent behaviorist John Watson, together with his wife, Rosalie, authored *Psychological Care of Infant and Child,* a popular book advising parents to treat children as "small adults." Here he wrote: "Never hug and kiss them, never let them sit on your lap. If you must, kiss them once on the forehead when they say good night."[18]

It is important to be kind to children, Watson explained, and equally important to treat them as objectively as possible. He described affectional responses as "mawkish" and "sentimental," and counseled parents to shake hands with their children in the morning and to give no more than a pat on the head for outstanding accomplishment of a difficult task. As for love, he explained:

> Remember when you are tempted to pet your child that mother
> love is a dangerous instrument. . . . an instrument which may
> inflict a never healing wound, a wound which may make infancy
> unhappy, adolescence a nightmare, an instrument which may
> wreck your adult son or daughter's vocational future and their
> chances for marital happiness.[19]

This book was reprinted as late as 1972, having already left its
mark on several generations of parents and children. Now we know
that hands-off parenting has negative ramifications whereas human
touch and physical comforting promote security as well as a wholesome sense of self. Moreover, we are aware of an entire spectrum of
interactional experiences that contribute to an understanding of the
self as unique and of the world as safe and nurturing.

Mirroring

Baby Nick, like all other infants, learns about the world through
nonverbal interactions. Held close to his mother, he hears her
rhythmic heartbeat, feels the warmth of her breath, takes in the
scent of her body, is soothed by her rocking motions, and looks at
her face. All babies use the expressions on mother's face as a way
of seeing themselves. While a mother holds her baby in her gaze,
he finds himself there, as if in a mirror. If she holds him "in reverie," he will experience himself as unique and worthy of her reverence. If, on the other hand, she is disinterested, depressed, or agi-
tated, her face will not validate his budding individuality.[20]

Indeed, babies internalize and reflect the moods of those in their
environment. They will appear worried and their bodies will tense
when people around them are irritable or sad.[21] Infants of
depressed mothers have been found to display more sadness and
anger than others.[22] In fact, the brain activity of such infants
between the ages of three and six months is similar to that of their
depressed mothers.[23]

An infant's experience of the world as safe and nurturing can be
easily displaced by a rush of troublesome feelings taken in from
the environment. In such instances, if his distress is not countered

with soothing, comforting human contact, he may be left with an impression of the world as antagonistic and nonsupportive. Moreover, he may be deprived of the energy needed to invest in his own self-organizing process.

Attunement

What happens *within* an infant as he organizes around a developing sense of self? Notably, psychoanalyst Daniel Stern finds that the infant's sense of self is significantly affected by his interactions with the caregiver.[24] A well-nourished self, as the seedbed for inner life and the organizing force behind development, provides the foundation for self-worth.

Self-worth, in turn, is linked to social relatedness as the infant moves through distinct stages of development. For example, in early infancy the baby prefers to look at faces rather than visual patterns, and vocalizes more while doing so. The four month old smiles, coos, and attempts to engage his mother through vocalizations, or when overly stimulated, averts his mother's gaze. Around nine months of age, the infant discovers that what goes on inside him are not isolated experiences. When confronted with strange or fearful situations, he will "read" his mother's face for signs of reassurance or alarm. He assumes that his mother has emotions like his own and that he exists in a universe of shared feelings.

Attunement—the mother's ability to understand her infant's feeling state and to relay her understanding back to him—validates the child's subjective experiences. This emotional resonance between mother and infant also tells him that his internal feeling states are widespread human experiences. To impart this understanding, the attuned mother will in some way *reflect* her baby's feeling experience. She may match the pitch of her voice to his squeal, or gently tap his foot each time he shakes his rattle. Stern gives this account of attunement behavior:

> A nine-month-old girl becomes very excited about a toy and reaches for it. As she grabs it, she lets out an exuberant "aaaah!" and looks at her mother. Her mother looks back, scrunches up her

shoulders, and performs a terrific shimmy with her upper body, like a go-go dancer. The shimmy lasts only about as long as her daughter's "aaaah!" but is equally excited, joyful, and intense.[25]

Ultimately, a parent's attunement behavior gives the infant a sense that others are interested in and willing to share in his feeling states. Seeing that others are responsive to his vital energy, he learns that he can trust his experiences.

The trusting infant then adds to his repertoire new perceptions, sensations, emotions, skills, and behaviors. His evolving sense of self subsequently organizes around expressions of his individuality—a uniqueness visibly treasured by the godlike beings who care for him.

Separation

Whereas Stern shines light on the interactive experiences that promote connection and consequently an emerging sense of self, psychoanalyst Margaret Mahler and her colleagues had a different focus in mind. In the 1960s while studying children from birth to age three, they wanted to learn about the child's capacity to successfully separate and individuate from his caretakers.

Healthy psychological development, said Margaret Mahler, hinges on a child's successful navigation through the intertwining phases of separation and individuation, a journey that begins when he is four or five months of age and ends when he is about three years old. Mahler termed this intrapsychic unfolding "the psychological birth of the human infant." *Separation* refers to the infant's gradual acquisition of both an inner representation of himself as separate from his mother and an ability to function independently of her. *Individuation* relates to the development of his own unique identity.[26]

Separation and Individuation

Let's take another look at Nick. When he is about four to five months old, his individuation begins physically as he scans his environment, testing the feel of objects with his hands and mouth.

When he masters reaching and crawling, he moves away from mom and starts relating to objects in a new way. Toys from her remind him of her and help him shift from mother-soothing to self-soothing and self-stimulation. Mahler, in keeping with object relations theory, would say that Nick uses these objects to symbolically satisfy his needs.

When he is between seven and twelve months of age, his memory development expands, enabling him to encode in his brain the image of his mother's face and his emotional responses to it. Soon he is able to recall her face when she is not present, use it to self-soothe, and with each repetition, further internalize the experience of an emotionally responsive mother.

As Nick learns to walk, sometime around one year of age, his territory expands. While covering increasingly greater distances, he checks back with mom to gain the sense of safety he needs for tackling ever newer turf. Great stores of energy propel him in his explorations as he practices his newly acquired motor skills. According to Mahler, when such developmental feats are on cue, the infant delights in discoveries and capabilities, and at the same time cultivates a variety of autonomous functions.

Rapprochement

Perhaps the most enduring of Mahler's concepts is that of *rapprochement,* a period beginning at about fourteen or fifteen months of age, as the realization of separateness becomes acute. Suddenly afraid that separating may lead to abandonment, Nick displays some very interesting behavior as he strives to be both united with and separate from mom. With the dual needs for connecting and separating at loggerheads, he begins to throw temper tantrums, rapidly swinging from one mood to another, whining, and reacting intensely when separated from mom. I am reminded of my first exposure to this stage when my two-year-old niece disrupted an entire household every day with demands for "chocolate (brown) socks." Toddlers by age two are grappling with a major dilemma: *how to be simultaneously autonomous and fulfilled (in the way that mother satisfies).*

The eighteen month old, meanwhile, is learning to coordinate these interrelated needs. Supporting his striving for rapprochement, a French word that means to bring together, is his parents' acceptance of his ambivalence and their ongoing demonstrations of love, which enable him to connect with self-soothing sources. The more deeply internalized his symbolic representation of the mother becomes, the better equipped he is to channel the aggressive energy of separation into goal-directed activity.

Shore adds another dimension to Mahler's concept of rapprochement by considering the role of shame and its impact on the nervous system during this period. Shame, an emotion known to us all, initially occurs when toddler behavior is interfered with by the ubiquitous *no* informing the child that it is not safe to run into the street, for example. At such junctures, the infant's physiology shifts from a state of "interest excitement" to deflation and low energy, marked by a motionless posture, aversion to eye contact, and—the hallmark of shame—blushing. Shame, Shore tells us, if handled well by the mother, facilitates development of the brain's frontal lobe by establishing an internal adaptation system to emotional negativity. In other words, just as the infant can call to mind a positive memory of mother for self-soothing purposes, he can also recall a memory of her reaction to forbidden behaviors. He can then curb his impulsive behaviors by anticipating his mother's responses to them—a necessary move toward social adaptation.

The child's capacity for internal shifting and remembering hinges on his repeated exposure to a caretaker who responds to shaming events, tantrums, and other misattunements by reinitiating eye contact and engaging in positive interactions with him. The more the caretaker activates this reunion activity, the more she fosters his ability to regulate his own emotions. Shame is therefore not only an unavoidable childhood experience but also an essential socializing catalyst available to assist the child as he bumps up against the grist of reality. The redemption of shame rests in the grace of emotional repair.[27]

So begins the movement into the final phase of the separation-individuation process. Between thirty and thirty-six months of age, Nick has internalized an image of both his caretaker and himself. Consequently, he begins to see the *world* as separate from himself. He is able to be alone and to comfort himself, for the soothing responses of his caregiver have become part of his repertoire of internal functions, as have responses for regulating some of his behaviors.

The True Self and the False Self

Parenting is not easy. Many mothers and fathers have unrealistic expectations of their developing child, and consequently grapple each day with feelings of disappointment. Some are more prone to exasperation, particularly if they have given little thought to their child's temperament, a factor that plays a critical role in the unfolding of personality.[28] Others—hampered by their own unmet needs, frustrated by the constant round of obligations, exhausted from sleepless nights, and lacking solid parenting information— are ill-equipped to cope with the demanding, unrelenting task of child rearing.

To the vulnerable infant, however, caregivers are all-knowing. They have the resources needed to ensure his day-to-day survival. And so he attempts to engage them in communication—an endeavor that may or may not prove successful. As we have seen, he is sensitive to their emotionality and will adapt to their needs and expectations at the expense of his own. If his caregivers happen to be depressed, emotionally remote, or abusive, he will alter his behavior to whatever degree is necessary to avoid further violation.

This adaptation to parental desires, moods, or demands gives rise to a disparity between who the child *is* and who he *must try to be*—or in psychological terms, between what pediatrician and psychoanalyst D. W. Winnicott termed the true self and the false self.[29] The *true self* is the seat of natural and spontaneous gestures, the source of creativity, and the aspect of the self that feels real. It is the essence within the infant that is acknowledged through the caretaker's attuning and attending behaviors. When the well-nurtured baby frets or fusses, his mother responds with wholehearted presence, committed to soothing and comforting him. When he laughs with delight in his game of peek-a-boo, his mother is equally happy.

This true self cannot blossom if the mother is routinely projecting fears and anxieties onto the infant, is clouded by depression, or holds unrealistic expectations of him. Psychoanalyst Alice Miller tells us that such a child "would remain without a mirror, and for the rest of his life would be seeking this mirror in vain."[30] As time goes on, we would see him designing postures of grandiosity to compensate for what was never mirrored back to his infant-self. He would be in constant need of endorsement and reflection from those in his environment.

The *false self* takes root as the child begins to identify with the parts of himself that please or soothe his parents, while disengaging from the parts of himself his parents disapprove of. The false self, in displacing the vital true self, generates a despair and narcissistic rage that often surface in pronounced behaviors. Alice Miller, for example, writes of a man who murdered 360 women. His mother had been a prostitute who, in addition to subjecting him to severe physical abuse, dressed him as a girl until he was seven years old. The cause of this man's life of crime may not be straightforward enough to be attributed strictly to childhood trauma and deprivation; nevertheless, "the simple and understandable despair resulting from his realization that he could never win his mother's love because he was a boy and not a girl" contributed its share to his heinous behavior.[31]

The psychological abandonment of an infant's true self parallels the physical abandonment described by Bowlby.[32] Abandonment depression sets in, and as time passes, the individual's life becomes permeated by a lack of satisfaction, numbness, and emptiness. Undifferentiated anger, a hidden companion to this state, is projected onto outside sources as ordinary frustrations begin triggering a deep inner rage. This rage is flavored with a desire for revenge, or for righting a wrong or undoing a hurt. Eventually, the person is apt to inflict on others the injuries he himself is most afraid of suffering, including the sadistic indignities he experienced at the hands of his parents.[33]

Empathy, too, is at stake. An infant deficient in experiences of attunement is likely to mature into an adult who is unable to experience the feeling states of others. Emotionally impoverished and driven by an underlying rage, he will attack others and have no feeling for what his victims suffer.

Rocking the Cradle

An infant's cradle needs to be rocked lovingly, consistently, and responsively. The bottom line in responsive parenting is the same whether it is presented through Schore's neurobiological lens or the words of D. W. Winnicott. Now recognized as one of the most insightful and compassionate parenting specialists of the century, Winnicott gave us the term "good enough" mothering.[34] The good enough caregiver, tuning into the communication loop between herself and her baby, senses the infant's needs and responds to them. If things go awry, delays occur, or distractions arise, the caregiver steps in and makes amends. This righting of wrongs (repair of misattunement) contributes to the baby's developing sense of trust in his environment.

Only from a base of trust can the infant venture into the unknown world of challenges or obstacles, and emerge with a secure sense of self. Allowing the realities of life to impinge uncensored on an infant is therefore ill-advised, for the self at this stage of development has not yet gained enough strength to negotiate such complexities. As the infant moves out of the arms of the caretaker and into exploratory activities, he needs the assurance of loving arms to return to.

Toddlerhood, with its struggle for autonomy, poses its own challenges. For one, the conflict between separating and connecting is likely to unleash a torrent of aggression. The good enough parent allows for the eruption, aware that this assertion of budding selfhood is in the developmental scheme of things. For another, frustrated over not getting everything he wants, the toddler is apt to scream out in protest. The knowing parent understands that attempts to silence the child will only prompt a power struggle

and short-circuit the valuable lessons to be learned about wanting
and getting. The child, in turn, loves the parent for allowing him to
express his feelings and be who he is. In essence, he feels love for
the outside world because his true self has been allowed to flourish.

A toddler's healthy sense of self is also nourished by the setting
of consistent boundaries. Parents who distinguish acceptable from
unacceptable actions foster this healthy self-concept by protecting
their child from harm and exhaustion. Hence, the child's needs are
not always satisfied and his wants are often thwarted; the resulting
tensions are nevertheless tolerable in an atmosphere that supports
frustrations, allows for emotions, and communicates the parameters
of appropriate behaviors in easily understandable terms. Surrounded by emotionally available and sensitive parents, such a child will
learn to self-regulate his emotions.

In a nonnurturing environment, the child's navigation through
developmental phases is at best precarious. A parent who does not
attune to her child, who blocks his attempts to explore, or who
strikes him for venting frustration interferes with the differentia-
tion process through the overloading of shame. Unpredictable and
unsupportive environments elicit stress responses in infants which,
if experienced over long periods of time, begin to infiltrate the
ways in which they express themselves temperamentally.[35] When
shaming is frequent and intense, the infant slips into a paralysis of
hopelessness, placing him at high risk for serious emotional disorders. He is likely to grow up with a poorly organized personality
structure and a compromised self-image, for the false self will
reign supreme.

Having internalized parental dislikes, contempt, or even hatred
for aspects of himself, he may turn these sentiments against his
disowned parts. As relationship specialist Harville Hendrix says:

> We hate ourselves for having needs that we were told were exces-
> sive or inappropriate, and for having traits that were hated by our
> caretakers. . . . Self-hatred is behind all the defenses. Its source is
> the presence inside our minds of a "bad" object, the internalization
> of the negative, rejecting parent.[36]

In condemning the attributes of his true self, the child is apt to cut lifelines to the creativity, vitality, and expressiveness that give meaning to his existence. Rarely will he comprehend that these rejections have little to do with who he really is and everything to do with his caretakers' inability to appreciate an energy that when allowed to flow naturally in early stages of life will neutralize itself. The good news is that these forsaken qualities will not have vanished. The tragic news is that without an appropriate context for their expression, they will remain dammed up behind an old wall of fear that the energy of spontaneity is unmanageable, or behind an archaic expectation that his own infants must quell their impulses of jealousy, rage, or defiance.

Attuning Journeys

Journeying provides a context for healing these early developmental wounds and establishing contact with one's true self. This is what I realized as I slowly and cautiously integrated shamanic concepts into my clinical work. I first suggested the shamanic journey to clients already familiar with ASC processing. Shifting from imagery and hypnotic trance sessions to journey work required only a few alterations on my part. In lieu of using my voice to induce an altered state, I played a drumming tape. I also instructed each client in the details of entering the lower world, requesting an encounter with a power animal, and presenting the animal with an issue of concern. Some clients later learned to journey to the upper world. In each instance a question for consideration was formulated from our therapeutic dialogue.

From the start I was captivated by two phenomena: an intense connection between the journeyer and power animals, and the journeyer's profound response to their nurturing behavior. Their presence spawned threads of both mirrorlike activity and attuning involvement that wove their way through each journey. Sometimes the attending behaviors elicited intense emotions, providing connecting experiences the client had lacked in earlier years. Other times, the response was more subtle, suggesting an encounter that was summoning the individual to higher levels of functioning.

The following client journeys illustrate these dynamics. The names of the journeyers have been changed, though the journeys themselves—spoken aloud while I transcribed them—remain intact.

Ramona

A woman in her mid-forties, Ramona was struggling with an unsatisfactory job situation. She had benefited from trance and imagery work in previous therapy sessions and welcomed the idea of using a structured shamanic approach for ASC processing. She described her journey with a tone of wonder in her voice.

I'm in a place with some reddish jagged rocks, golden cottonwood trees, and a river. I feel drawn to the rocks behind the trees. Now I'm touching them—they feel cool, rough. Looking for a crack in the rocks, I see a dark spot, so I go to it. It's a kind of opening . . . dark inside. I'm going down a narrow passageway. The rocks here are damp. I see a light ahead of me, and small trees. The sky is a very light gray. "I'm looking for my animal." I don't see any life right now, other than the trees. Water is flowing by. Pushing aside the tall grass, I come to a stream with big rocks. "I'm here if you want to come out. I want to meet you." I see—oh, a beaver. "Beaver, are you my animal?" Actually, he just said he was. I don't know why, but he's making me laugh. He's splashing his tail around. What a funny guy! [Laughing] Now we're dancing together—kind of skipping and dancing and somehow holding hands.

He wants me to follow him, so we're cutting through the grass. He's ahead of me, moving toward some rocks on a small hill. Now he seems more serious. He wants to show me his family up by a rock surrounded by debris. He's beckoning me to go in there, but I'm not sure I can fit. I'm shrinking down so that we're the same size. He wants to show me something in there. OK, I go in—but all I see is a small nest. Nobody seems to be around.

This is so strange—I think he wants to have a smoke with me. He's got a pipe and wants us to smoke together. [Inhale-exhale] It feels really good to be here sharing something very special with

this animal. [Inhale-exhale] It feels comforting, and I'm not thinking about anything else. He seems to be my friend and wants to
help me. I really like this beaver.

My surroundings are dropping away—everything seems relevant, pure, simple, as though I'm in the center of something really
protective. [Inhale-exhale] Beaver puts his paw on my arm. It feels
really gratifying. [Crying] This animal isn't talking much, but
being here with him makes me think that we are of one mind, that
a lot can be said. It feels good to be in this space.

He's going outside, back to the stream. I need to go back up.
The drum is beating fast. I say good-bye to Beaver. Climbing over
rocks, I head for the dark crack. I see light ahead and come out by
the big, wide river with yellow trees.

In Native American traditions an animal is said to bring medicine to an individual who calls upon it, medicine being "anything
that improves one's connection to the Great Mystery and to all
life."[37] Each animal brings its own kind of medicine and the
beaver—the "doer" of the animal kingdom—is believed to bring the
gifts of family, home, industriousness, and determination. Beaver
signifies the sense of accomplishment that comes with applying
oneself to a task.[38] How poignant it is that an animal carrying medicine for doing and accomplishing should reveal itself to this woman
who was having difficulty realizing her creative potential![39]

Even more noteworthy is the protection, safety, and trust
Ramona felt in the presence of her power animal. She expressed
the immediacy of her connection with Beaver both verbally and
through her tears. Inhaling and exhaling symbolize the ebb and
flow of life; inhaling represents nourishment of the physical self,
whereas exhaling demonstrates release. The ritual of pipe smoking
is akin to the sharing of breath—that is, of life and spirit. Pipe
smoking among Native Americans is considered a sacred act
undertaken with the intention of calling forth power for good outcomes.[40] For Ramona it was a sharing of life and an invitation to
reawaken portions of her psyche.

Ramona's history suggests a lack of attachment in early childhood. She has few memories of her childhood prior to age five.

Her mother, killed in an accident when Ramona was six years old, had had a difficult relationship with her husband. Ramona remembers her mother as a strong, engaging woman who "changed when my father came home—she seemed to take care of his needs out of duty." After her mother's death, Ramona tried to fill the woman's shoes by becoming a caretaker to her father, a pattern that persisted into adulthood, accompanied by episodes of depression. Both Ramona and I believe that her initiatory journey installed a sense of alliance and comfort that contributed to the healing of a developmental breach incurred in her childhood.

Now, over a year since her first journey, Ramona is interacting with several power animals in her shamanic travels. She is vitalized. And she is preparing for a new profession—one that will engage her creativity in a satisfying way. With a sense of accomplishment and direction, Ramona has brought closure to this piece of therapeutic work.

Andrew

Andrew, a professional in his forties, came to therapy hoping to overcome his unwillingness to trust, which was interfering with his marital relationship. He knew that the inability to trust a loved one is traceable to early formative experiences deficient in consistent and attentive caregiving, and his intent was to address this flaw.

Having made effective use of processing while in a hypnotic state in an earlier round of therapy, Andrew responded favorably to the suggestion of journeying. In this, his first journey, he entered the lower world through a rocky outcropping that opened onto a spiral stone stairwell, which he descended. Emerging into a meadow with several paths, he chose the one directly in front of him and invited the appearance of his power animal.

> I continue down the path, and standing by a clearing in the woods is a huge white buffalo bull. "Are you my animal?" Bull nods yes, paws the earth with his right front hoof, turns, and walks into the clearing as though he expects me to follow. I see another white buffalo and a calf. "Are you my animal?" They walk over to the large

bull. I have the idea that all three of them want me to come visit them.

I plunk down in the grass next to a body of water. I feel comfortable, safe, and peaceful. I want to nestle with the white bull, and I tell him that. He moves his body into a semicircle, and I snuggle my back against his side. The other two circle around us. I could stay here forever. [Sigh] I feel tears—not from sadness, but from being welcomed home to a safe place. The drumbeat is like the heart of the buffalo . . . steady, constant, powerful, omnipresent. I have no cares, no desires; it's just wonderful to be here.

Andrew's opening journey, like Ramona's, provided a deep sense of safety and nurturing. Nestled against the buffalo, Andrew felt at home, reminiscent of the unity and merging experienced by a baby nestled in mother's arms.

In the animal medicine tradition the appearance of a white buffalo signifies both prayer and abundance. Its medicine is "prayer, gratitude and praise for that which has been received," portending "a time of recognizing the sacredness of every walk of life," including those different from one's own. Part of the buffalo's message is to "honor another's pathway, even if it brings you sadness."[41] Andrew, it seems, was being challenged to consider the ways in which his wife's path was at variance with his own, and to respect her path while attending to whatever sadness this may have aroused in him.

Buffalo abundance—as reflected in the presence of a buffalo family, rather than a single buffalo—signals a time of plenty, and in this instance an abundance of buffalo nurturing. Being tended to creates connection and begets trust, the quality Andrew believed he was most in need of. Furthermore, the appearance of white buffalo, often considered the most sacred animal, may have been heralding a more abundant spiritual connection for Andrew.

The white bull's physical nurturing was repeated in subsequent journeys. When Andrew asked the bull how to move into a more intimate marital relationship without compromising his own individuality, he was told that he needed more courage.

I sit down with him again, and we're doing a ceremony in which he is letting me feel his heart. [Pause] It's hard for me to grasp this right now, and I'm criticizing myself for being wimpy about it. Buffalo communicates telepathically that we will do the ceremony again and again till I've gotten it. And meanwhile, I'm not to confront my wife or try to resolve any big issues. First I have to have my buffalo heart.

In this ceremony I ask if I can snuggle up to him again. Yes, he says, and I can feel his heart coming through my back into my body as the sun keeps us warm. Taking my buffalo heart will be a huge step—major things in my life will change. There will be no compromise about anything important to me, and right now that's scary.

I feel like I've failed today—I should have been able to claim my buffalo heart right away. I'm sad and depressed, like at other times in my life. I feel lighter when I say that. Buffalo raises his head and gives me a little smile. "Yeah, you're getting it," he's telling me. With this insight I feel better, less sad. Maybe when I'm depressed, I need to start snorting, running, jumping, doing a buffalo dance, just to feel that kind of energy. When I'm in a depression, I get totally mired in it, it weighs me down. But now I feel lighter, because I know what sadness is about and what to do for it.

In this journey, revealing an evolving relationship with a power animal, attention was given not only to nurturing activity but to Andrew's concern. In his offering of courage—"heart"—Buffalo triggered several underlying dynamics. Andrew, feeling ill-equipped to fully claim the courage, slipped into self-criticism over his lack of readiness. He acknowledged the sadness he felt and linked it to his self-criticism, later identifying it as a pattern with developmental roots. Buffalo validated the insight. Andrew's mood shifted as he began to focus on physical activity—a tried-and-true remedy for depression.

Buffalo "contained" Andrew's moods with quiet acceptance and no hint of pressure or judgment. And within the boundary circumscribed by the bull's calm presence, Andrew was able to tap into a deeper understanding of his depressions: the infant, whose ability to trust was impeded by a distracted mother, had carried sadness and self-criticism into adulthood.

Perhaps most remarkable is the fact that with no input from me as the therapist, Andrew was able to garner both insight and healing energy within twenty-five minutes of entering this altered state. He had managed to circumvent resistance and quickly beat a path to his own resources. Here we see how journeying enhances the secure therapeutic relationship.

Upon concluding this work on trust and courage, Andrew left therapy and continued journeying on his own. Some months later, he returned. I was struck by the many changes he had undergone. He was living more from a heart of courage. He and his wife were exploring core issues in their relationship. And although he was still afraid to confront their differences, he was committed to resolving them. Andrew continues to utilize journeying as an anchor, a wellspring of nourishment and connection, and a gateway to wisdom.

Jerry

A retired professional, Jerry had struggled all his life with the remnants of a childhood that had us both convinced his parents used John Watson's book as their primer. He described his childhood as "emotionally sterile." His parents, who valued intelligence and performance, were too preoccupied with personal interests to spend time interacting with a curious and would-be adventurous child. My sense was that his infancy left him starved for touch and sensitive interaction.

Jerry named his child-self Wilbur, an epithet he associated with "ineffectual." As his parents engaged in shouting matches, Wilbur would cower, and he carried this feeling of helplessness to school, where he was quickly targeted by bullies. In therapy Jerry frequently processed material while in an altered state of consciousness, visualizing Wilbur as "stuck halfway between home and school" with a knot in his stomach. To this day Jerry struggles with an undiagnosable pain in his diaphragm.

Jerry was eager to give journeying a try. Very soon he had acquired several power animals as well as an upper world teacher. Here is an account of one of his later journeys.

My intent in this journey is to become more intimately acquainted with Wilbur. I'm in the meadow, and I find the tunnel, go through the musty passageway, walk down the steps to the door, and there's Raven. He nods his head. I say to him, "I want to do more with Wilbur," and even now as I say this name, it's very difficult. Raven says, "That's fine. Let's go."

We go to the street corner where Wilbur is sitting. Wilbur says, "I have trouble with this name. It's like I'm defeated before I start. I don't know what to do now." Grandfather (a teacher from the upper world) is in the background. He has a soothing presence and immense power. Grandfather says, "Why don't you hold Wilbur in your lap for a while?" I pick Wilbur up, sit down, and hold him in my lap. Wilbur starts to cry. Raven is sad, and Bear (another power animal) cries. I ask Wilbur, "What does it feel like to have that name?" Wilbur says, "My chest hurts. I feel weak. I don't like being around people, because I am afraid they will ridicule me." We sit quietly.

Grandfather says to Wilbur, "Why don't you listen to the name 'Wilbur' and dwell on that for a bit?" [Long pause] Wilbur comes up with a word; *shame*. Now he's spelling out *w-e-a-k*. Grandfather asks Wilbur to go back and touch the word *shame* again. "Three things are there," says Wilbur, "*shame, weakness* in my chest and stomach, and it all rests on a *dull anger*." Grandfather says to dwell on the 'weak.' [Pause] "I have a sense of *fear*," Wilbur replies. Grandfather says, "That's quite a collection: shame, weak, dull anger, and fear."

I ask, "How are you doing, Wilbur?" Wilbur says, "This is hard, and I don't know what to do with it." Grandfather says, "Let's shove back the dull anger, the weakness, and the fear, and stick with this shame. What comes?" Wilbur says, "It's like someone telling me, 'Shame on you for being alive!' I had to go to school. I have to go home. I want to run away where it is *safe*." I can feel Grandfather's love. I can feel Bear's anger. I can feel Coyote. Coyote has power. I'm not ready for him yet. [Sigh] Wilbur continues: "I used to get picked on. I remember one kid called me 'Jew-boy.' There was no way I could get back at them—or protect myself from them, or from my parents. The worst is weakness." [Sigh]

I tell Wilbur he is doing great. I hug him. He hugs me and says, "I want to work on *weak*." Coyote says, "Yeah." I say that I'm going to let all this stew around inside me until next time. Raven says, "That's good." So I take Raven inside me, and I take Wilbur inside me, and I take Coyote inside me even though he starts laughing, and I take Bear inside me. I smile at Grandfather. Back to the door I go, waving good-bye, and through the tunnel to the meadow just as the drumming accelerates.

Here journeying complemented an already installed therapeutic format. In earlier sessions Jerry had identified the fearful child within him and had used the technique of focusing.[42] Elements of this approach surfaced when Grandfather instructed Wilbur to "dwell on" a feeling.

Jerry—an anxious, shy man accustomed to internalizing his feelings—had never before acknowledged the shame embedded so deeply within him. Certainly, he was assisted in this realization by his cadre of support: Bear, Raven, Coyote, and Grandfather, each of whom responded with compassion. Bear cried for Wilbur, angry that he had been treated so miserably; Raven felt sad; even Wilbur cried. Jerry, however, unable to plumb the depths of emotional intensity, could do no more than sigh. Connecting to painful feelings is a central challenge in Jerry's work, and to his good fortune, the power animals were showing him feelings he had yet to explore.

Two aspects of this journey are particularly intriguing. One is that Wilbur is given the opportunity to experience attunement. His sadness and frustration are reflected in the expressions of the animals supporting him. Jerry, meantime, experiences a glimmer of self-generating power while Coyote, now introjected, prepares to move into a position of greater potency.

Secondly, Jerry is not asked to push beyond his level of readiness. He appears to have within him a form of knowing that, once tapped, brings forth *wisdom* in directing him toward wholeness. This journey, in bypassing me as the therapist, led Jerry not only to a deeper understanding of his dilemma but to self-empowerment and hope for recovery. Healing work, Jerry understands, is a process, not an event. Committed to Wilbur's integration, he continues to journey, both at home and in sessions.

Heather

Heather is a fifty-year-old artist whose college-age children recently left home. She entered therapy strongly motivated to "move into" her muse with more assertion, yet obstructed by early parental injunctions that devalued spontaneity and creative expression. Aware that her parents had given no credence to her artistic vision, she felt hampered by an "emotional hangover that says I'm not good enough to manifest what I want."

Knowing that Heather had a strong affinity for nature and a passing familiarity with shamanism, I suggested journeying as an appropriate tool. Although she had no trouble contacting a power animal, she found the journeying format awkward. So we abandoned this approach in favor of hypnosis and a verbal exploration of her issue. Even so, she would periodically refer to the power animal and express a desire to "get to know it better." I remained focused on the material we were processing, for a great deal of content was emerging with regard to her parents' attempts to control their two children and her own feelings of isolation as a youngster. After several more sessions, Heather went on vacation to a beautiful remote area of the country. One night while there, she had a life-changing dream experience.

> I was in a funky cabin in a rural setting. My mother was screaming and abusing two dogs, perhaps burying them underground. I became partly conscious and thought to myself, "I'm having another terror dream in new form. I don't have these dreams anymore, but here I am with one. What can I do?" The idea came that there was something out there to help me—oh yes, the power animal. I called for Lizard, and not wanting the fear and repulsion of my dream to overtake me, I watched him. He was there for fear, and that is how I ignited the meaning of Lizard. Then everything changed. I had the power to deal with the dream.
>
> When I woke up the next morning, I felt OK. I knew that even if I had this dream again (she has not), I had the knowledge and power to deal with it. I never felt so resolved. Having the knowledge of what Lizard is, I felt transformed forever. Lizard is my source of help, my security.

Heather achieved her therapeutic goal. Empowered to move in a creative direction, she advertised her artistic wares and was rewarded with glowing reviews. She now has several power animals. "They are a resource I turn to when I'm feeling anxiety," she explains. "I evoke the power of the animals."

Heather's experience shows both the profoundness and the subtlety of shamanic influences. Her earlier work had apparently prepared her to take on Lizard's power so that she could stare down fear and horror when the need arose. Heather's process, like those of other clients, was guided by an inner rhythm and, while operating beyond her conscious awareness, activated healing impulses.

The Elements of Healing

How does journeying bring about these changes? To begin with, journeying occurs in an altered state of consciousness similar to the adaptive ASCs induced by hypnosis and other therapeutic modalities. While moving into a journeying state, the individual exhibits physiological changes characteristic of an altered state: facial muscles relax, rapid eye movement may commence, and the voice may soften as speech slows down. Focus is fixed on the unfolding experience. Very soon the rational mind falls silent, awareness of the outside world fades, and the individual proceeds to describe activity that is unexpected, illogical, and rich with symbolic imagery. Primary process thinking comes to the fore as animals speak, quadrupeds fly, mountains shrink, and rivers run red.

Grounded in a secure relationship with power animals and upper world teachers, the journeyer participates in an unfolding story. Everything in the journey—each image, each activity—has meaning. And although the symbolism here, as in dreams, may not be immediately understood, the imagery that arises relates directly to the individual's situation.

The power animals play a key role in the developing motif by holding and reflecting the emotions of the journeyer, mirroring inner states in a way never before experienced by individuals with insufficient nurturance. Because of an animal's devotion, the journeyer comes to feel valued and attuned to. Internalizing this attunement, she leaves the journey with an acute sense of the animal's presence, which she is able to awaken in her everyday reality. Stated in object relation terms, *the experience of a consistently attentive figure becomes internalized and anchored in consciousness, where it serves as a nurturing reference furthering the completion of developmental tasks.*

The journeyer, who can at any moment evoke an awareness of the power animal within her, may in times of fear or emotional turmoil turn to this for fortification or for movement toward developmental resolution. Realizing that her power animal had become actualized in her phenomenological world, one client said: "It's not a matter of thinking about the animal all the time, or even realizing it's there. It's simply knowing that the connection to the power animal is available when I call on it. This 'knowing' fills me with the energy of connection and protection."

Adequate bonding is the birthright of every human being. Attachment figures provide a matrix of support, attunement to feelings, and guidance in acceptance of self, tolerance for mistakes, and enhanced understanding. From this secure base we dare to venture forth and learn about the world. Deprived of such a base, we strive instead to fill the void. We search for a perfect mate who will fulfill our every need, or we seek out an endless supply of material goods, or stalk one guru after another—none of which can repair the disconnected state within.

Journeying, however, can. Why? Because the shamanic cosmos provides *surrogate energies for the bonding experience,* no matter how many years have passed since the deprivation made its mark. These energies enfold the journeyer whether she has embarked on her own or in a therapeutic setting. I refer to the interweaving of shamanic methods and psychotherapy as Shamanic Psychotherapeutics. Journeying in this context, as illustrated in the foregoing examples, brings profoundly healing energy to psychological dysfunction and potent salve to the scars left by developmental wounding.

Little Red Riding Hood
Meets the Wolf

*The shaman and the psychologist, now sleeping under the tree,
begin to dream. The shaman sees himself in the lower world, enjoying
the night sky. The moon illuminates the profile of a badger digging
a hole in the earth. The shaman marvels at the ferocity of its
strength. The psychologist, in her dream, enters an art museum
and begins studying Edward Hicks's painting,* The Peaceable
Kingdom. *Although puzzled and intrigued by the calm repose of
the animals, Quakers, and Native peoples portrayed in the kingdom,
she is drawn to the stare of the lion.*

IN THE PREVIOUS CHAPTER WE EXPLORED SOME OF THE WAYS IN WHICH
journeying brings nurturance to developmental wounding,
addressing the first question posed in the prologue to this book:
How does shamanism help heal early emotional wounding? Now
we turn to the second question: Can journeying be a vehicle for the
release of pent-up anger?

Anger—a combined feeling of tension and hostility—often
leads to aggressive behavior that is destructive to other people or

to oneself. The nature of this aggression, how it manifests in our developing years, and why it poses such a challenge to society has long been a focal question for humanity. Even fairy tales such as *Hansel and Gretel, Snow White and the Seven Dwarfs,* and *Little Red Riding Hood* touch on the threat of violence. *Little Red Riding Hood* is especially revealing, for here the innocence of childhood is literally gobbled up in its encounter with violence. While not discounting other interpretive spins on the tale, we can zoom our lens onto the wolf as representative of the destructive tendencies of human nature, and see if another destiny may perchance await the young heroine.

Aggression

Many people believe the human drive toward aggression and destruction is instinctual and self-fulfilling, and given the flagrant displays of violence so evident today, it is small wonder that they do. Believing in this "built into our genes" aggression that leads unavoidably to violence, however, foreordains our course as a species and serves to appease the individual and collective guilt provoked by its expression. That is, if humankind is by nature destructive and will eventually meet a violent demise, we need not atone for aggressive violations or attempt to forge peaceful resolutions . . . and we need not concern ourselves with why Little Red Riding Hood was eaten by the wolf.

By Nature or By Nurture?
Are human beings naturally destructive? If so, do we have within us the capacity to counteract these forces? Several theories support the notion that instinct is responsible for the destruction and savagery perpetrated by humans. British naturalist Charles Darwin maintained that rage is the drive needed for survival.[1] German ethologist Konrad Lorenz hypothesized that human aggressiveness is evolutionary and essential to preservation of the species.[2] Sigmund Freud attributed aggression to impulses coming from the id, the seat of life and death instincts. The goal of all life, he said,

is death. And aggression, a derivative of the death instinct, is essentially the inclination toward self-destruction turned outward onto others. Because the id is amoral and illogical in its drive to satisfy needs, the realism of the ego and moralism of the superego are required to dampen its pressing energy. The eruption of violence is, in short, the id's announcement of its instinctual tendencies.[3]

Anthropologist Ashley Montagu offers a different perspective: he asserts that aggressive behavior is learned. The learning of aggression, he says, accompanied the evolution of higher mental functioning and was influenced by the cultural milieu. Simply put, as early humanity began to cluster in groups, the structure of the brain started to change. Montagu states: "As we trace the details of man's evolutionary history we see that it is with the development of culture that man's brain began to grow and develop in a simultaneous feedback interaction with culture as an organ of learning, retrieval, and intelligence."[4]

Montagu also points to the ongoing role of social context learning. No matter where aggression is studied, whether in cultural groups, social classes, or religious settings, "the story is everywhere the same: aggressive and nonaggressive behaviors are mainly learned," he explains.[5] He goes on to suggest that children who witness or are subjected to aggression in their homes, learn to be violent.

The truth is that the nature-versus-nurture controversy is best resolved when we adopt a nature-*and*-nurture perspective. We know, for example, that males have higher testosterone levels than females, and that from the beginning of life they exhibit more aggressive behaviors. Indeed, brain imaging procedures show that in a relaxed state, males demonstrate more activity in the limbic system—the "reptilian" part of the brain that activates survival responses such as aggression.[6] We need to acknowledge both this reality and the demonstrated capacity of human beings to learn and to make informed choices about their dispositions and actions.

Does *genetics* play a role in the tendency toward aggression? Jerome Kagan, a psychology professor at Harvard University, in a longitudinal study of 600 children, presents evidence of an inherited basis for inhibited and uninhibited temperaments.[7] Inborn dispositions for specific styles of behavior do contribute to personality, he tells us. While inhibited children are more likely to be fearful, shy, anxious, and proficient in internalizing their feelings, uninhibited children are more likely to be outgoing, fearless, and adept at externalizing their feelings. Furthermore, aggressivity is more often associated with the behavior of uninhibited children.

Although Kagan implies the existence of a genetic underpinning to behavior, he discounts disposition as a primary factor in determining human conduct. He believes the right use of will overrides temperamental bias, emphasizing that although an individual has no control over the emergence of an emotion, she does have control over the ensuing action. Kagan says, "Put plainly . . . every sane adult of average intelligence has the ability to moderate his or her asocial actions."[8]

So we see that from a genetics perspective some children are more predisposed to aggressivity. At the same time, mounting evidence supports the impact that learning can have on aggressive behavior. It follows that uninhibited children can learn to moderate their emotional responses. What they need is guidance in exercising their options—all the more so if they witness aggression in their surroundings.

Turning to the nurture perspective, we find that aggression need not be destructively self-fulfilling. Social psychologist Carol Tavris, in organizing data from social and biological research on anger, has made clear distinctions between aggression and anger. Aggression is an expression of rage in response to the threat of harm, and it is related to our primate heritage, she concludes, whereas anger is a human emotion subject to a wide range of expressions. "Human anger," she notes, "is not a biological reflex like the sneeze, nor simply a reactive display designed to ward off enemies."[9] It is a feeling that crops up in either the presence or the absence of external stimuli, arises from the recollection of disturbing incidents, can be sustained for years, and can be feigned when it does not exist. To help us cope with the hostile thoughts, feelings, and impulses that pepper and plague us, she recommends a variety of approaches ranging from cooling-down techniques to the development of new habits and skills.

Victor LaCerva, a physician specializing in public health, delineates forty steps that can be taken personally and collectively to help decrease the levels of violence in our nation.[10] These steps, like Tavris's guidelines for contending with unbridled anger and nagging frustrations, take for granted the human capacity to exercise choice and control.

If human aggression is to some degree instinctive, then departures from hostile, acting-out behaviors must be attributed to learning. Mastery of some sort must account for societies in which violence is minimal or absent, for the fact that one man kills his opponent while another praises the strength of his foe, and for the passivity of a soldier out of touch with his "killer tendencies."[11]

Researchers know one thing for sure: the moderation of emotional responses does not come easily to individuals who have been maltreated in childhood or have witnessed repeated acts of violence. In 1991 psychologist Michael Mahoney, after extensively reviewing studies of parental abuse and neglect, concluded: "The evidence is now considerable that these dysfunctional patterns of parent-child interaction are (1) frequently related to patterns of emotional distress, self-abuse, and psychopathology in the family, and (2) often perpetuated across generations and through spouse selection."[12] Moreover, in a 1994 report on intergenerational aggression, exposure to family violence was predictive of male aggression across three generations.[13]

Developmentalists Dante Ciccheti and Sheree Toth add more fuel to the fire with the results of their comprehensive review. They point out that physically abused children, as they mature, not only are more likely to inflict violence on others but are at greater risk for psychopathology. Concurring with Mahoney's conclusion, they state: "Taken as a whole, research on the attachment relationships of individuals who have experienced maltreatment during childhood suggests a potentially life-long pattern of maladaptive interpersonal relationships."[14]

As we have seen, the newborn's interactions with her environment mark the beginning of adaptation, and from that point on, complex interactions with her caretakers generate a specific manifestation of her inborn potential. So it appears that despite the "encoding" of aggression, the environment of the developing infant plays a crucial role in her later demonstrations of violence. Behavioral patterns, personality traits, and the expression of potentially aggressive tendencies are all influenced by the attitudes, modeling behaviors, and responses of her caretakers. Clearly, the need for informed, child-wise parenting has never been more dire.

The Developmental Picture

Aggression *is* a fundamental drive rooted in our basic biology. Although it at times manifests as hostility or destructiveness, René Spitz told us that "by far the largest and most important part of the aggressive drive serves as the motor of every movement, of all activity, big and small, and ultimately of life itself."[15]

The energy of aggression is discharged through the muscular apparatus of the body.[16] The hungry infant's wails, punctuated by the kicking of his legs and the flailing of his arms, discharge energy and support his survival by attracting the attention of his caregiver. Similarly, the exertion of muscle groups propels the movement toward autonomy as the crawling babe engages in his to-and-fro dance with mother, and as the toddler runs from mom in the dart-and-shadow pursuit of individuation.

During the period of rapprochement, the toddler's struggle to be close to and separate from his mother constitutes a dilemma he cannot yet put into words. The thwarting of his emerging will by the powers that be can only be expressed through his body. To learn that his personal desires cannot always be fulfilled, he must encounter parental firmness, accompanied by an acceptance of his inevitable outbursts. Parenting expert Alicia Lieberman remarks: "This is why temper tantrums are so important for healthy development. Tantrums take a child to the very bottom of his being, helping him to learn that anger and despair are part of the human experience and need not lead to lasting emotional collapse."[17]

While experiencing the naturalness of the aggressive feelings that course through his body, the maturing toddler is learning that the external world of action is distinct from his internal world of feelings and thoughts. In time he develops capacities for remembering, fantasizing, and reflecting, thereby realizing the options available to him in moments of frustration. He may beat a toy drum, for example, bounce on a trampoline, line up toy soldiers for a fantasy battle, or negotiate with his parent for an acceptable means of satisfying his wants. In one way or another, his body becomes involved in the sublimation of energy and subsequent neutralization of the aggression. The child discovers that while feeling hatred or a desire for destruction internally, he need not act directly on these impulses and can instead discharge the aggressive energy through other activities. As soon as he has experienced the repair of misattunement and finds that he is able to hate his mother without destroying her, he feels safer and his love for himself and for her deepens.[18]

Thus, the drive toward separation requires as much parental acknowledgment as the drive for connection. Dismissing its influence, ignoring its purpose, or lashing out each time it makes an appearance will hamper the child's mastery of a force that brings wholeness to life.

Psychoanalyst Beata Rank, who speculated on environments that balance the competing drives of connection and separation, wrote, "We may be able to modify or even eliminate the destructive element of aggression."[19] When a child is treated abusively or observes parental acts of aggression, however, acting-out behavioral patterns may follow him into adulthood. In such environments the impressional and ripening self absorbs the imprint of violence. Here, too, as Montagu reveals, the role of learning serves its purpose—albeit an unfortunate one.

What Should Little Red Riding Hood Do with the Wolf?
Countless individuals full into their adulthood are limited to one degree or another by developmental woundedness, which can reveal itself in dysfunctionality of all sorts, including bestial behav-

iors. These adults parent children who are destined to repeat the maladaptive patterns. The sins of the father are indeed visited upon the children—but by virtue of *imprinting*, rather than by way of the gods, as Euripides suggested.

Coming to grips with our nature, for both our children's sake and our own, is a major life task. We like to believe that intellect rules our behavior, that wisdom guides our actions, yet the ongoing tension between our unfulfilled needs for bonding versus selfhood can sabotage our best efforts—at which point our developmental gaps reveal themselves. A father who champions good parenting, for example, may one day physically assault his rebellious adolescent son, unaware of the unresolved tension that has been lurking within *him* ever since his unsuccessful attempts in adolescence to separate from his own parents. Triggered by his son's behavior, his own aggressive tendencies come to the fore.

How can we help our children cope with this aspect of their nature before it wreaks havoc in their lives? The answer rests with a Little Red Riding Hood we have not yet met. In the original tale, the innocent protagonist enters her grandmother's house and finds in her bed a deceitful wolf. Using his mental prowess, the cunning creature tries to overcome the child. She succumbs and he eats her.[20] When we regard the wolf as representative of both parental rage and the internalized wrath of the child, we begin to wonder: Is being swallowed alive the fate of a child who loses her voice of assertion to the growls and shouts of her parents? If so, how can she learn to subdue the "wolves" in her life so as to avoid having to either project her destructiveness onto them or sacrifice her individuality to them?

A different future awaits a contemporized Little Red Riding Hood who is secure in herself and no stranger to her own aggression. Blessed with parents who did not curtail her individuating energies in toddlerhood, she has felt the "motor" of life supporting her developmental journey toward resiliency, and she is familiar with the scent of challenge. Encountering the wolf, this heroine knows him to be who he is (*not* her grandmother) and decides to use her power to tone him down. Taking the pepper she has in her basket, she throws it in his face and leaves the premises!

But the wolf—like other beasts—has more than one side to his nature. Although a carnivorous aggressor, he also shows himself to be intelligent, humorous, and family oriented. In the wild, too, the wolf exhibits strong familial ties, mating for life and living in a pack while pursuing individualistic urges. The late scientist Carl Sagan and his wife, writer-producer Ann Druyan, attest to the dual nature of animals. In tracing the lineage of the human species, they point out that our animal ancestry informs our humanness, and that primates, in particular, are not merely barbaric, for they are capable of demonstrating friendship, altruism, attachment, loyalty, courage, intelligence, innovation, inquisitiveness, and fore-sight. Sagan and Druyan write: "Those who deny or decry our 'animal' natures underestimate what those natures are. . . . And if our intelligence is our distinction, and if there are at least two sides to human nature, shouldn't we be sure to use that intelligence to encourage the one side and restrain the other?"[21]

These two researchers join the ranks of those who maintain that behavior is influenced by learning. Psychologist Z. Y. Kuo, they inform us, showed that kittens who view their mother killing and eating a rat will almost always demonstrate the same behav-ior, whereas kittens who are reared in the same cage with a rat but never view a cat killing a rat, will almost never kill a rat.[22] Sagan and Druyan remark: "Of course humans are not cats. But we might be tempted nevertheless to guess that childhood experi-ence, education and culture can do much to mitigate even deep inborn proclivities."[23]

Daily, new findings by developmentalists are dispelling old notions about infancy and childhood. As a result, many Americans now recognize that infants' needs are *not* primarily physiological and that children do *not* need to be "tamed" into compliance. We are beginning to grasp the impressionable nature of the infant's psyche as she reaches out for connection, validation, and encour-agement to be who she really is. We are starting to understand the wounding of the vital self that occurs in response to a lack of touching, lack of interaction, or outright abuse. We are even begin-ning to see a link between these deprivations or exploitations and the rage vented daily in businesses, homes, schools, parks, and streets. Learning, we are discovering, plays a pivotal role in the altering of behavior, just as healing does in the assuaging of psychological pain.

Individuating Journeys

Frustrations, resentments, and repressed anger can all be processed while journeying. Moreover, journeyers are capable of learning contained, appropriate ways to release aggression. The following clients' journeys, each of which approaches anger from a different perspective, set the stage for overcoming previously obstructed developmental hurdles.

Doug

Doug had a history of alcohol and drug abuse, and was a Vietnam War veteran. During the war, he held a desk job and never handled weapons. His sleeping quarters were bombed one night, killing his roommate and injuring others with whom he had worked. Doug escaped injury and continued living nonviolently, with one exception. Several years after leaving the army, he experienced the collapse of what he called an infatuation. Feeling jealous, he went on a rampage in his apartment, taking an ax to his furniture.

The incident of destruction terrified him. He felt he was "on the verge of a psychotic breakdown," and the next day he was sure the world was "falling apart." His concern was not that he would harm anyone else, but that he would go crazy or kill himself. He had no frame of reference for this upsweep of rage, and no understanding of its implications.

Doug began therapy with me about ten years later, complaining of job difficulties. By that time he was sober, having had a spiritual "peak experience" that turned his life around. Not only did he refrain from ever using alcohol or drugs again but he fell in love and married a woman to whom he had developed a strong commitment. When I first met Doug, he was mild mannered, deferring, and lacking in life force. He related a history heavily influenced by childhood illness, traditional religion, a "John Wayne" father, and a caretaking, invasive mother. Yet despite his oppressive upbringing, he had made great strides in coming to terms with his addictions and in establishing an intimate relationship.

While working with me intermittently over a period of several years, Doug found ASC processing of great benefit. When journeying was suggested, he readily adopted this approach. Upon mastering the technique, he began using it to process issues between sessions. Immediately after one of our sessions, he realized that the flu symptoms he was experiencing mimicked an illness he had had prior to his dismissal from a previous job. Consequently, Doug formulated the following question to take into his next journey: "How can I rid myself of the energy left from the N— Corporation?" The next day, he mailed me the transcript of a taped journey, with a cover page that read, "Caution—extreme violence appears in the content of this journey."

I enter the tepee and descend a ladder toward the light below. I send out a call to my power animal and the others (additional power animals and spirit helpers). Wearing buckskins and with my pouch tied to my waist, I stride out of the cave entrance. I walk confidently toward the clearing in which I see all my journey friends gathered. I raise my arm in greeting. They sound a welcome and pull me into their circle.

At the center of the circle my old boss is staked out on the ground. He is wearing his usual white shirt, tie, and slacks. "Can you tell me what this is all about?" he asks. "Can't you guess?" I answer, but figure he never thought about it. "I know I made some mistakes," he says, "but this is a little extreme." I reply, "I don't think so."

I sit on the ground beside him and look into his face. I hear my friends grunting appropriately. My power animal is at the north; a younger version of myself, at the south; the old man (a spirit helper), at the west; and I am at the east. "I do want to say that I've been able to do wonderful things since we parted company," I remark. "So I thank you for that. I returned to school and graduated with two degrees as the top graduate student in my department." Boss asks, "Why am I here? Sounds like everything worked out just fine." I reply, "Well, we're here because no matter how things worked out, I still feel a whole lot of resentment, anger, and even hatred toward you for what you did. I've decided I'm not going to carry that cancer around with me anymore." Boss responds, "OK, so dump it and let me out of here."

I reply, "No, you don't get off that easy. First, I want you to know how much it hurt me when you screwed me over. It took me a long time to look myself in the eye and not see a failure. You robbed me of a career I spent fifteen years building. You robbed me of a profession I thought I loved. Because of you I had to change my entire life, and no matter how good it may be now, it hurt like hell! I trusted you. I trusted that other son of a bitch (Boss's assistant) you told me to trust."

Out of the corner of my eye I see two male figures holding the man who had been Boss's assistant. My friends must have anticipated what I had not. I point to Boss and Assistant. "You two screwed me. You set up artificial criteria that had nothing to do with how I did the job I was hired to do, and you judged me not good enough to be in your organization—and I am still pissed at both of you." I stand up and walk over to Assistant and look into his eyes. "I trusted you. You knew the pressures and you went along with Boss's plans to get rid of all the men that Level II hired. A lot of good it did you after the big guy left. Got the ax yourself, didn't you? Got anything to say for yourself?" "I don't know what you're talking about," he says, looking away. "Sure you do, Mr. Assistant. I got the shaft because of your people and your mistakes. But would you stand up for me? No way. You just sucked up, like always."

I nod at the two men. They strip off Assistant's clothes and hold him. I look at Boss, who's trying to keep his eyes shut. Someone comes and holds his eyes open. "We'll make this fast, Mr. Assistant," I say. I pull a knife from my belt, grab Assistant's penis and testicles, and slice them off. The men force his mouth open. I smile. "Here, Mr. Assistant, suck on this!" And I shove his genitals into his mouth till he gags. Assistant is crying, and is trying to scream but unable to. "Don't talk with your mouth full, Assistant." Assistant is bleeding and turning pale. I nod and the men holding him allow him to fall to his knees. "Now watch," I say.

I walk over to Boss who does not look at all well. "Boss, tell me again how sorry you are about everything that happened. You're a good Catholic boy—you know how good confession is for the soul." He responds, "I'm really sorry. I was a terrible administrator. I screwed up. I'm sorry." I respond, "See, now don't you feel better? And for your confession, we'll give you a little penance." I pull square nails from my pouch and pound them into his wrists and ankles. "And just for good measure . . ." I nail his penis to the ground between his legs.

Assistant is being forced to watch, but he grows paler. "Stop this," Boss says. "Please, just stop this." "We're not done yet, Boss. You gutted my career. It's only fair that I do a turnabout for you." I take my knife and slowly slit his skin open, about half an inch deep, from his pubic bone to his breastbone. I then lift away the flaps of skin and ask him to look, but he won't. I nod and one of the men lifts Boss's head. He wretches. "It's not over yet, Boss." I take a hatchet from my belt and proceed to sever each of his arms and legs until his torso is limbless. I bend over Boss's face and, nearly nose to nose, look him in the eye. "Good-bye, Boss." I lift my hatchet and sever his head just as he is about to scream.

With my right hand, I pick up his head by its hair and turn it so that he can see from overhead what his body looks like. I bend down and, with my left hand, pull his still-beating heart from his chest and hold it before his eyes. "The next time you think about fucking someone over, you remember this, Mr. Boss." I summon Raven and place Boss's still-conscious head on the nail at his penis. Raven walks up to him, plucks out one horrified eye, and nibbles on it while the other eye watches. Raccoon says she wants the other eye and works at getting *it* out.

Assistant watches. I look at him. "Good-bye, Assistant." I plant my hatchet firmly into his skull, producing the sound of a baseball bat hitting a ripe watermelon. He falls and we place his body on Boss's.

The old man comes over to me and puts his hands on my shoulders. "Is your anger gone, my son?" I reply, "It is, Grandfather." "Do you feel remorse over what you have done?" "No," I answer somewhat surprised. "Good. We will send their spirits back to them and rid our land of their stench." Grandfather claps his hands and the circle attends him. "Is there anything you want to say to Doug?" My younger version steps toward me and puts his hand on my shoulder. "You are a warrior. We will be one." My child-self now appears and says, "I am proud of you. You are the man I want to be." Power animal growls from his position as the circle reconstitutes itself. "It is a sad thing for a man to carry this much anger and pain for so long," says Grandfather. "It is a glad thing that you carry it no longer." All the others grunt and nod approval to everything that is said. Two other power animals belch.

Grandfather squats and mutters words as he pulls two large pieces of flint from his pouch. "We have called these spirits here to rid our friend of misery. They injured him in ways they did not know but now do. Perhaps they can find healing in this new knowledge. We send them back to the sky and the world from which they came." The old man leans over and strikes the pieces of flint together, creating a large spark. The bodies catch fire like magnesium and incinerate almost instantaneously, along with all the blood and flesh. There is no evidence that anything occurred here, except for the circle of animals and spirit helpers.

I go in turn to every member of the circle and place my hands firmly on each one's shoulders and look each one in the eye and say thank you. When I am finished, we walk back toward the cave. I give each one a hug. Grandfather raises his hand to me as I walk out of the light to return home. "It is a good day to live," I say. I return to the ladder, climb up to the tepee, and step into this world.

What transpired in this journey was out of character for Doug, in terms of both his ordinary life and everyday experience of himself. His commentary at the conclusion of the journey began with, "This is *shocking* to me . . ."

Acts of violence are nothing new. In the Judeo-Christian tradition, Cain's killing of his brother, Abel, was followed by a succession of feuds and wars instigated by the desire for blood vengeance. Ancient cultures worldwide practiced primitive forms of torture long before more elaborate methods were developed by civilized nations in Europe and Asia. In the Middle Ages, both church and state applied torture to extract information from prisoners or to change their religious beliefs. As psychoanalyst Erich Fromm has pointed out: "Men were castrated, women were dis-, emboweled, prisoners were crucified or thrown before the lions. There is hardly a destructive act human imagination could think of that has not been acted out again and again."[24]

Nor is the shamanic world free of brutality. In the initiate's journey described in chapter 1, the shamanic ancestors pierced the initiate with arrows, cut off his flesh, tore his bones out, and counted them. The archetypal motif of destructive aggression permeates every dimension of our existence from the seismic punches of earthquakes to the mortal combat of warring nations.

Doug's journey, we must remember, is about the release of long pent-up rage. It was a fury harbored not only by an adult male unduly dismissed from a valued position but also by a postadolescent male exposed to atrocities in Vietnam, an adolescent boy oppressed by a militaristic father unwilling to acknowledge the sensitivity of his artistic son, and a child infantilized by a mother unable to cope with the childhood illness that confined him to his bed for months at a time. Approaching midlife Doug, having assumed a submissive response to many of life's vicissitudes, was in need of the energy that lay buried beneath his resignation. Expressing anger and aggression was not part of his life equation. In fact, as a sick child he had been told that if he did not comply with the doctor's orders, he would die, as did a relative who had had the same infectious disease. He had been trapped in a double bind: if you want to survive, don't act upon the natural urge to express emotions.

The intensity of the rage in Doug's journey is a measure of his continual burying of impulses and desires to strike out against authority and against the contingencies of fate. Compliance—the recommended prescription for survival—was a pattern he took into adulthood; strapped into a passive mode, he became incapable of mobilizing energy to redirect his course. As his therapy unfolded he came to recognize his fury, which culminated in this journey of release. Here, without harming himself or others, he encountered his aggressive shadow, allowed for its expression, and in so doing, reclaimed the energy of his vital self.

Reclamation for Doug, an individual so repeatedly constrained by tyrannical people and conditions, involved primitive rage. Castration, although it has many symbolic meanings, categorically denotes the deprivation of masculine strength and power. This stripping of virility is what Doug experienced when he was fired from his job—a dismissal that most likely recapitulated his childhood dynamics with an authoritarian father, a mother invested in keeping him in a childlike state (an investment that I believe existed prior to his sickness), and an illness that robbed him of vitality and opportunities to engage in age-appropriate assertiveness. The revenge motif is seeded in a narcissistic rage born of the tyranny imposed by the false self over the true self, of the thwarting of vital essence when one is too young and vulnerable to fight back. This rage is split off from conscious awareness, unable to avail itself of the developmental experiences needed to neutralize its force. It was not the adult Doug who annihilated his employer and the assistant; it was this split-off energy that had festered and pressurized in its disconnected state.

Some theoreticians believe that the repeated release of anger reinforces a habitual acting-out of violent emotions. They point to the temper tantrums of kindergartners, the nightly rages of alcoholic parents, and the angry tirades of domineering spouses. This concern is not to be dismissed. Some individuals, including tantruming four or five year olds, are in dire need of learning to intercept and redirect aggressive energy. Others such as Doug, however, must learn to *identify repressed anger* and *find appropriate channels for its expression*. In either case, journeying provides a therapeutic container.

During expressional release in psychotherapy, the client is in need of compassionate support, not interpretation or intellectual scrutiny. Furthermore, the expression of intense feeling is more likely to facilitate change when: (1) the emotion is conflict laden, has been avoided, or has not been consciously known, (2) the client deems the emotional expression personally meaningful, and (3) the evocation of affect is subsequently processed therapeutically.[25] Doug met all three of these criteria: aside from the furniture-destroying event, the expression of anger—let alone violence—was antithetical to his style of behavior as well as his way of thinking; he not only found the journey experience meaningful but marveled at his assertiveness and his placement of personal boundaries; and he followed up the journey with therapeutic processing. As a result, he underwent a dramatic change.

This is how Doug now contrasts the furniture incident with the violence of the journey.

> It was frightening when I took the ax to the room. I didn't know anything like that was in me, and I knew nothing about the release of anger. The journey experience was entirely different. By that time, I'd had enough work in therapy to know that I carried toxic residue. I knew that my intensified use of drugs and alcohol after Vietnam dampened my feelings of rage about the war. In the journey I was given permission to seek revenge. It was the violence of the emasculation that was so cathartic, so healing. I had to do to the perpetrator what was done to me.

The difference between Doug's aggressive display of destruction with the ax and his release of rage in the journey has to do with *intent* and *containment*. Only in the journey was his aggression accompanied by a conscious intent to heal and kept within the confines of curative circumstances. And hence, only in journeying did the mending of wounds, both developmental and situational, transpire.

Doug's affinity for journeying sustains a process that no longer needs the support of regular psychotherapeutic sessions. He is established in a new position of leadership, which he fulfills with confidence and authority. He has moved from passivity to activity, defining his life not in terms of what the world is doing to him, but by assessing situations and making informed choices that resonate with his deepening sense of self. Among the many elements contributing to his new growth were his contact with power animals and spirit helpers, as well as the terrain of the journey. Doug describes his experience of journeying in this way:

It was essential to the integration process—a method I want to continue to explore and to use. It is real to me. It's someplace I go to, not something I make up.

Helen

Not every confrontation with frustration or anger elicits violent release. For Helen, the medium of journeying offered subtle and gradual support for a multitude of stressors, including physical pain from an automobile accident. Concerned about her slow rate of healing, she began a dialogue with her power animal, focusing on her inability to express anger and deal with her resentment. In a subsequent journey her power animal responded to her concern with the following message:

Look at your expectations. Lots of anger and resentment comes from failed expectations, from grasping at things that don't work out. When they don't happen, they cause disappointment and anger at the self or at others. Maybe in the future you can feel less anger and resentment if you don't have such expectations, especially for perfection.

Do not be afraid of others' reaction when you express anger. If you say you are angry about something, say it with intent to clear the air rather then to fossilize the anger into resentment. With clearing there's a mountain slide, a clap of thunder, and that's all right. The creek just keeps moving and doesn't dam up simply because of a rock slide. There's a class of things truly intolerable to be angry about. Rather than turn them into resentments, make some kind of decision to change the situation.

You have to have some courage to be angry. You have to be willing to understand, or try to understand, the other person and let go of expectations that aren't reasonably founded on what the other person can do or be. Disagreement comes out of profound miscalculations about who other people are.

Never before had I heard Helen talk this way. She presented herself as a perfectionist with preset notions about right and wrong ways of doing things, along with a strong penchant for criticizing herself when outcomes fell short of expected results. Over time, her simmering resentments had fueled an anger that she would not express for fear of violating her code of conduct.

This journey addressed three facets of Helen's dilemma: difficulty in expressing anger, resentments resulting from misplaced expectations, and a need to alter intolerable situations by solving problems and prioritizing her options. The power animal presented interpretations I had not yet discussed with her, unsure if the timing was right. Content targeted by the power animal must have been on cue, however, because our postjourney discussion brought to the surface the genesis of her perfectionistic standards—a father who measures performance against a set of rules poorly matched to Helen's present life situation. Information that comes directly from the client's processing, I have found, is far more beneficial than information issuing from the therapist.

When hostility and resentment interfere with well-being, some clients, like Helen, come to therapy to learn nondestructive responses, while many, like Doug, come to learn how to acknowledge and mobilize the energy into life-affirming expressions. Common to both these quests is the movement toward individuation.

So we see that journeying can be a powerful conduit for releasing and exploring anger, since it brings to the surface sources of childhood energy that for survival's sake have remained unexpressed. These early interferences in the developmental task of separation must be addressed if we are to replace today's rampant violence with a healthy management of anger. As for the next generation, let us set our sights on permitting Little Red Riding Hood to outsmart the wolf.

The Alchemical Connection

The shaman and the psychologist continue their sleep, their dreams deepening. The shaman, in his dream, meets with a young initiate emerging from a period of fast and isolation. Together, they dance around a ceremonial fire. The psychologist, dreaming of a client gripped by uncertainty about a compromised future, feels the man's anxiety spilling into the therapy room. She is challenged by the need to both reflect his apprehension and guide him into a state more receptive to options. She envisions him relaxing by a stream— his favorite setting.

WHAT IS THE DIFFERENCE BETWEEN THE HUNGRY BID FOR ATTENTION IN a family distracted by other concerns and the call for support in a psychotherapy session? What is the difference between hostility openly expressed in a park and the rage vented in a journey?

The primary difference is that the cry for attention and the hostile behavior are uncircumscribed, whereas the call for support and the rage of the journeyer are bounded by an intent to heal. Being bounded by an intent to heal implies first, the individual's *desire for remediation,* and second, the therapist's and the journey beings' capacity to *hold* and *protect* the thoughts and feelings that come to expression in their presence. While on one level each of these healing disciplines offers security, comfort, insight, and an opportunity to release individuating energy, or aggression, on another they provide containment and ultimately the potential for transformation.

Containment

Simply put, to contain is to hold and protect. The mother contains the infant in her arms. The therapist contains the processing client. Spirit helpers and power animals contain the journeying client. And each of us contains our individual feelings and experiences. How containment is manifested throughout our unfolding development can spell the difference between a life that is satisfying and connected and one that is despairing and isolated.

The Therapist As Container

Some time ago I was given a handblown glass vessel. Measuring about twenty-nine inches tall and forty-two inches around its belly, with a neck narrowing to a three-inch opening, it now stands in my office, a visible reminder of what this phenomenon called psychotherapy is all about. Guardian of containment, it ensures that whether a client is immersed in dialogue, delivering a straightforward release of feelings, practicing assertion skills, or deep into journeying, he will be "held." This large blue vessel serves as a visual reminder that, as a supervisor once explained to me, the moment I close the door behind an entering client, I am symbolically committing to the containment of all that spills forth over the course of the session. Simply put, the psychological holding and protecting of a client rests in the hands of the therapist—hands that we hope are not only strong but capable of drawing and sustaining good boundaries.

Attunement. In the original containing relationship, the mother who holds her infant absorbs his expressed emotions and, in order to respond in a meaningful way, decodes them. She learns to discern the cry of hunger from the howl of pain and wail of exhaustion. She tunes into his discoveries and acknowledges his frustrations. If such a holding environment is not present in infancy, we know what happens—the child grows up looking to later relationships for restorative containment.

Some of these "grown-up children" come knocking on the therapist's door and, stepping inside, enter a domain in which the nuances of containment are formatted in psychological expression. Psychoanalyst W. R. Bion explains that the therapist acts as a container for the client by "intuitively understanding and transforming [his] communications, including [his] projected unconscious anxieties."[1] When the therapist contains, she empathically acknowledges the client's vicissitudes. Seeing beyond the dilemma to his wounded being and listening with both her mind and her heart, she relays back to him her understanding. This segment of the communication loop, although often nonverbal, conveys gentle acceptance to the self-condemning client and compassion to the grieving one.

When a client feels attuned to and relaxes into the realization that the therapist can hold the pain of his struggle and not be shattered by it, he risks taking a closer look at the troubling contents of his inner life, sharing his discoveries with the therapist and accepting her support and guidance in return. The more he learns to transform his capacity for intake and output, *the stronger his container becomes.* Healing and redemption of vitality follow. The same is true for Shamanic Psychotherapeutics. In Doug's journey we saw how the power animals' attuning behaviors fostered his articulation of deep pain, detoxifying and transforming his projected aggression.

Serving as a container for another person's process is a complex task. Ask any therapist, or anyone else you know who frequently provides an empathic ear to family members or friends. The most common hazard is that the listener can become emotionally hooked.

In such instances caretaking reactions may arise: "I won't let this happen to you—I'll help you out of this mess." Or judgments may crop up: "I told you last year that you were headed for disaster with this idea."

To successfully contain another person's process, one must balance objectivity and subjectivity. Therapists have an advantage in this regard, for they do not interact with their clients on a daily basis; in addition, they have presumably been trained in the practice of containment. When a client relates a problem to me, for example, I must assess his situation clinically, prioritize difficulties, identify suitable approaches, and remember that the dilemma pertains to *his* life story—*objectivity*. At the same time, I must be able to hear the emotions underlying his delivery and let him know I understand his feeling states—*subjectivity*. Properly balanced, these functions promote the feeling of safety that is needed to contend with the vulnerability of a distressed or regressed self.

Furthermore, the timing of interventions is of paramount importance. If I suggest an approach or exercise while a client is still testing the safety of the therapeutic waters, his container may wobble or crack. Only when I have correctly gauged his degree of readiness is he apt to feel protected and grounded in a sustained in-vivo self-exploration with me.

The art of containment does not stop with the balancing of cognitive and feeling functions and the timing of interventions. For transformation to occur, the therapist must also have a vision of the client moving into wholeness. Such a vision rests in the belief that the human organism not only has the capacity for reconstituting and healing but is *designed to exercise* this capacity. How is such a vision conveyed? By silently acknowledging that we are so much more than meets the eye, that the client seemingly tethered to the past and present has within him the resources to begin moving toward an empowered future.

This perspective is similar to the healing vision sustained by shamans. The containing therapist, like the shaman, knows that although physical disability may be irreversible, emotional struggle a necessity, and death inevitable, how the person orients himself toward challenge and physical demise lies within emotional and spiritual domains. The therapist sees behind the shelter of mind and body to a soul on an excursion to disowned and isolated parts of the self. Such excursions are sometimes accelerated, sometimes slowed, and at other times "stalled in the station." While the therapist supports the client in his current predicament, she also envisions him whole and healed. She may silently invoke an image of him as sound in spirit and secure in selfhood, effectively containing and relating to his different energies; or she may silently call on her own power animals to assist in the healing containment.

A therapist who has succeeded in laying the groundwork for a trusting relationship with a client may wish to introduce journeying, in which case it is essential to first assess the client's level of functioning. Some clients are not suited to journeying. Noncandidates for this type of ASC include individuals who are in acute grief, who are dissociated, who demonstrate or have demonstrated psychotic symptoms, and who are unable to concentrate. Others may try journeying but find it awkward or incompatible with their psychological state. Still others may have no desire to embark on a journey. In some instances, a lack of interest in journeying reflects the therapist's inability to provide suitable containment—a deficiency that the sensitive therapist will note and correct.

The Role of Emotions. Since the therapist's job is to contain, she must recognize emotions in whatever form they may arise. Like flares, emotions attract attention to the turmoil brewing within the client, although he himself may disregard, ignore, or minimize them. The word *emotion* is derived from the French *movoir*, meaning "to set into motion" or "move the feelings."[2] I like to think of an emotion as "energy in motion"—energy that moves because it is seeking expression and wants to be in motion.

But what do we do? For one thing, we see emotions as good or bad—good when they arouse delight and trigger helpful behaviors, and bad when they are markedly disturbing or apt to prompt hurtful behaviors. For another, we wall them in, fearful that if expressed they may create chaos for both us and society.

At the core of sound mental health is the realization that emotions are *neutral*, without valence in either a positive or negative direction; that the longer we wall in emotional energy, the more forceful it becomes; and that we are in charge of how we *act* on our feelings, *channeling their energy into either creative or destructive* endeavors. This realization of choice marks the dawn of self-awareness, awakening an understanding that we can learn how to release emotional energy in ways that will not harm ourselves or others.

Cognizant of these realities, a therapist sensing a feeling state in her client sits with it while knowing that it may be only the tip of a long-frozen emotional iceberg beginning to melt. Crying over the death of a friend may indicate the presence of unresolved grief over past losses. Test anxiety may point to worries about correct performance dating back to years spent with a demanding perfectionist. In journeying, strong feelings may emerge long before they are verbalized. Affective testimonials such as tears, smiles, yelps of surprise, laughter, or profound silence provide springboards for postjourney discussions.

Resistance. We are all, to one degree or another, resistant to exposure and change—a tendency that can be acutely experienced in therapy sessions. The client container may appear difficult to fill or hard to empty; some containers are easily broken, for their sides are too thin, their openings too small, or their handles missing. A client sensing the muscle of repressed energies is apt to be terrified that these emotions, once tapped, will be unleashed with annihilating force against everything in the environment, including the self. He may worry that his connections with others will be forfeited and his existential dread of isolation and aloneness borne out.

For some clients, the thought of giving vent to long-buried and smoldering rage calls forth visions of being forever condemned to a burning inferno. For others, it evokes fear that their internalized attitudes of scornful parental figures which have thus far been projected onto others will give way to a gripping sense of self-hatred. (It is much easier to fixate on a neighbor's bigotry than to painfully acknowledge our own contempt for others.) To defend against such outcomes, a client will often choose to keep pockets of "threatening" energy sealed off from his conscious mind.

A containing therapist, in addition to untangling this confusion, holds the resistance and honors its protective function. Sensing the magnitude of a client's repressed grief, for example, along with the degree to which a backlog of feelings interferes with his functioning, she will focus on strengthening his container. An overeager therapist, on the other hand, will be quick to interpret the underlying dynamic, forgetting that too much input too early may cause the client to flee. As container of the client container, the therapist must exercise caution and avoid resorting to techniques, including journeying, when the client most needs *assurance* and *emotional support.*

To strengthen her own container, a therapist may choose to take the issue of containment into her personal journeys. Any time I am hooked by a client's story, feel the punch of my own struggles while listening, or fail to detach after a session, I know a journey is in order. During one such voyage I was shown that the flamboyant, spontaneous nature of my client was resonating with a disowned part of myself, causing me to bristle internally whenever she described certain of her behaviors. The antidote: paying more attention to my playful impulses and carving out time to do so.

The Client As Container

Unaccustomed to thinking of ourselves as containers, we may not suspect that when our feelings are out of kilter or our emotions interfere with effective relating, our containing capacity has been compromised. Arriving at the therapist's door, we hope for understanding and meaningful insight into our impasse. In the best of all worlds we will receive more than that.

Client containing capacity, it turns out, is often obstructed, weak, or otherwise imperiled. For example, one client may say that he cannot "take in" feelings or information; despite a yearning to be filled, he may have sealed himself off from emotional input because of past physical or emotional violations and a resulting inability to know who he can trust. Another client may be stymied by an unpredictable and uncontrollable outpouring of feelings that occurs from time to time, or by his emotions suddenly sinking into inexpressibility. Both situations require a therapist well versed in container fragility. Clients who are emotionally supported by such a therapist increase their capacity to withstand vulnerable states, thus building for themselves a more resilient container.

The Journey As Container

Journeying takes containment a step further (in fact, a client once described moving into nonordinary reality as a "session within a session"). First, journeying relies directly on the wisdom of the client's unconscious. Rather than requiring the therapist to outline a journey progression, it invites client and therapist to carve out feasible questions *together,* after which the client takes into journey the one most resonant with his needs. A client with repressed grief, for instance, may ask: "What would be helpful for me to know about my lack of energy?" or "How can I bring more motivation to my work?" or "Why do I feel overwhelmed by simple tasks?" With experience, journeying clients become adept at composing questions on their own.

Second, journeying queries prompt shamanic responses as open-ended as the questions themselves. I may think a client is in need of X, only to learn that the power animals lead him to Y, and appropriately so. Answers from the journey beings come in various ways—through shared activity, words, or demonstration. As in dreams, the responses are at times literal and at other times veiled in metaphor. Disguised invitations for a client to move more deeply into problematic areas are accepted only if he is ready to take the plunge.

Third, the movement and insights triggered by shamanic interaction emanate from the client's psyche, not from the therapist's interpretation or assessment of symptoms. And because the biddings and cues arise from within the client, they are more readily "owned" and acted upon. Throughout the journey, the client is in charge: he not only decides on the question to take in with him but consciously chooses whether or not to engage in the unfolding activities, aware that exiting the journey is always an option.

For the therapist, the beauty in this technique is that the healing endeavors are inaugurated *by the client*. Negative transference (a projection onto the therapist of unconscious feelings originating from dysfunctional interactions with childhood parental figures) is reduced, complemented by a great deal of healing transference onto the power animals and other journey beings. In other words, the client experiences these beings as nurturing. From the therapist's chair, this displacement of transference is likely to be looked upon with welcome relief, as is the new role of *collaborateur*. Together, therapist and client invigorate the mechanism of change by establishing the journey format, appreciating the resourcefulness of the power animals, and celebrating the potency of shamanic healing.

In the end, the most significant outcome of journeying is the self-empowerment of the client. Some prospective clients, reticent to enter therapy because of dependency concerns, are heartened to learn of the degree of control available to them in journey processing. Others, searching for methods that can be sustained after therapy has ended, are inspired by the lifelong applications of this approach; while instructing a client prior to his first journey, I emphasize the long-term nature of the relationship he is about to initiate. Journeying is a staple of mental health: *it targets problems as they arise and, when practiced regularly, strengthens weak links in the psychological immune system.*

Moreover, it can be interwoven with other techniques such as Eye Movement Desensitization and Reprocessing. In targeting abusive situations during eye movement work, clients who have an established relationship with a power animal often bring the strength and protection of the animal to the painful content that emerges. Here, too, the diminished transference onto the therapist results in self-empowerment, increasing the strength of the client's container.

Transformation

Although journeys manifesting aggression can call forth horrendous displays of violence, the fury does not spill over into ordinary reality. Such journeys are not to be confused with sorcery, invocations, or the placing of curses; to the contrary, their healing intent offers individuals a context in which fear of reprisal for pent-up rage can be overridden and neutralized. This healing intent allows one to grieve over injuries never warmed by the mending heat of anger, ultimately leading to an integration of vital aspects of the psyche.

Moving past the barriers of protection into the accumulation of repressed pain calls for a container capable of enduring great intensity without exploding. Well primed by the containing therapist in conjunction with the power animals, this inner container, the *journey container*, can become as refractory as a crucible. The compressed feelings within this vessel may then begin to stir, generating a heat that ignites an alchemical transformation—alchemical, because it transforms crude emotions into refined awareness.

So it is that while journeying takes place on one level, a form of alchemy transpires on another. The journeyer enters the domain where shamanism and psychology meet. The alchemy he experiences there, the internal link between these two realms, inspires a change that generates well-being.

Alchemy, an occult science of long-standing tradition, was practiced in China and India before the birth of Christ. As arcane as its practices may seem, images of wizards mixing metals in foaming test tubes miss the mark. Alchemists prior to the 1600s did attempt to convert base metals into gold; however, they also sought to "perfect everything in its own nature," including humankind.[3]

The alchemists' pursuits entailed collaborating with nature and focusing on gradual, persistent change such as that exhibited by plants sprouting from seeds and diamonds emerging from coal. Their intent was to accelerate natural processes, and although they were thought to have effected some metallic transmutations, their most tangible contributions set the stage for modern chemistry. For us today, alchemy endures primarily as a metaphorical model for psychological work—the perfection of human nature.[4]

The process of perfecting the psyche is currently known as *individuation.* Jung, who studied alchemy extensively, described individuation as the means by which a person becomes psychologically whole while gradually integrating into consciousness the contents of the unconscious mind. As this occurs, the lowly aspects of life are transformed into more noble ones.

Alchemical imagery pervades the shamanic dimension. The world for the alchemist, as for the shaman, is alive with all things "interpenetrated and animated by a living spirit."[5] For example, a tree, signifying growth, symbolizes Hermetic philosophy, which underlies many of the early alchemical writings. In the shamanic domain the tree is equally symbolic: the Cosmic Tree, or World Tree, is said to rise from the center—the umbilicus—of the earth, with its upper branches reaching toward the heavenly deities. Eliade wrote that the tree, "expressing the sacrality of the world, its fertility and perennuality, is related to the ideas of creation, fecundity, and initiation, and finally to the idea of absolute reality and immortality. . . . It represents the universe in continual regeneration."[6] The tree is in fact one of the most common representations of the shamanic axis connecting—and providing entry into—the lower, middle, and upper worlds.

Alchemical growth is "pre-eminently concerned with the seed of unity which lies hidden in the chaos," Jung told us, referring to the human's movement toward wholeness.[7] Central to this movement is the archetype of the child. Here the Jungians have their own way of saying what we was described in chapter 3: portions of the self lost in the wake of early emotional wounding must be restored. "The child," said Jung, "is all that is abandoned and exposed and at the same time divinely powerful. . . . an imponderable that determines the ultimate worth or worthlessness of a personality."[8] Emerging as new life out of the darkness, the child represents the coming forth of the individuated self. So it is that through the union of opposites, the light of conscious awareness illuminates the darkness of the unconscious mind, the banished comes together with the realized, and the buried energies of the child-self become yoked to the energies of the acceptable self. In each instance the "good" is coupled with the "bad." The flowering of the child archetype redeems the personality, bringing it to a higher stage of realization.

This new life is, in Jung's words, "the most precious fruit of Mother Nature,"[9] the wondrous answer to the either/or dilemmas that bind the conscious mind. He often alluded to the midwifing role of nature in such alchemical births, particularly in the contexts of dream and ritual. But at one point he went further, stating, "Nature, the world of instincts, takes the child under its wing [where] it is nourished or protected by animals."[10] Here Jung described the alchemical transformation that we know transpires in journeys.

Alchemy provides the recipe that takes us to the "gold." Our task is to find equivalent ingredients and procedures. To transform matter, the ancient alchemist applied heat and moisture to the metals within the crucible. To bring an individual into fuller expression, the psychotherapist constructs a safe setting capable of containing the heat of the client's conflict. Whereas the alchemist of old tried first one oxide and then another, the psychotherapist explores a series of ideas. Integral to both procedures is trial and error, stops and starts, and a combination of inclusion and exclusion. In effect, participants in both labors collaborate with nature and thereby become cocreators.

The movement toward both perfection and wholeness unfolds incrementally. Medieval alchemists spent years in isolation, grinding, mixing, melting, distilling, and fusing. For transformation to occur, the substance had to be corrupted; a more weighty gold, for example, required the addition of certain oxides. A similar adulteration is called for in the gradual movement from dysfunction to integration. In this process, heretofore unknown archetypal content disrupts the psychological status quo, propelling the individual to become who he authentically is.

This is precisely what occurred in Doug's individuating journey. Shamanic beings formed a circle (offering containment) and lit a fire (prompting transformation). Urged on by the permission-giving activity of Doug's shamanic guides, the emotions of his unacceptable self surged to the fore. Released through the grueling actions of his regressed self and contained by the animals and spirit helpers, these baser aspects of his nature merged with his more virtuous qualities, and consequently became transformed. The holding here, as in the alchemical crucible, served two invaluable functions: it prevented leakage of the expressed energy into everyday life, and it contained the heat of the discharge—the heat needed for transmutation to occur.

Illuminating the Unconscious Mind

Psychologists explain how the contents of the unconscious mind move into the light of awareness. Shamanic journeys demonstrate this movement. The journeyer takes questions to his spirit helpers and harvests the images they evoke, which he records in his journal and ponders with his therapist.

Archetypal Images

Jungian theorists tell us that instincts, or basic drives, of the collective unconscious manifest in archetypal images, as we saw in chapter 2. Archetypes are preconditions of life that "not only reach upwards to the spiritual heights of religion, art and metaphysics, but also down into the dark realms of organic and inorganic matter."[11] Everything we know of in life has an archetype—mother, father, hero, trickster, birth, rebirth, death, power, magic, the wind, the sun, the moon, trees, animals, and other aspects of nature, as well as ideas and attitudes.

Each archetype is bipolar, composed of psychic opposites that connect backward (into physical and primitive realms) and forward (into intuitive and spiritual realms) while encompassing obscurity and clarity, as well as good and evil. The mother archetype that emerges from the unconscious, through imprints of mother exposures, is conspicuously dichotomized: the good mother is clear in her intuitive nurturing and spiritual protectiveness, whereas the evil mother manipulates veiled forces to serve her own needs at the expense of her child's. When the mother figure fails in her nurturing obligation, an impression of the evil mother begins to form within the psyche of her child. It develops, like a photograph, from the "negative" of the mother archetype.

In journeys that provide nurturing and healing, we discover archetypal expression in its most promising form. Mother representations include objects, sites, or beings overflowing with fertility and fruitfulness—such as springs, trees, gardens, forests, or helpful animals.[12] The beaver in Ramona's journey offered her comfort and protection, and hence, although masculine, might be considered a mother archetype. So might the small cave into which she was led. The same can be said of the buffalo that gave Andrew the feeling of being "welcomed home."

In the context of journeying, the mother archetype invigorates developmental growth—a phenomenon that occurs in the following way. An infant deprived of maternal attunement will experience activation of the bad-mother archetype. This negative image is all that is available to him, for the infant's psyche is too undeveloped to manifest an internal nurturing archetype and his environment does not reflect an external one. With physical maturity and journeying experience, however, he becomes able to access nurturing archetypal energy. Once a nurturing image is in place, the journeyer is able to proceed, if need be, to the next developmental task of separation and of articulation of banished childhood feelings. In my experience, such cathartic journeys do not transpire until one has a safe and protective connection with a spirit helper or power animal.

Jung described archetypal images as "systems of readiness for action."[13] Hidden within the depths of the psyche, they are charged with joy, sorrow, fear, love, hate, and all other feelings of phylogenetic origin. In the immediate vicinity are emotions associated with more contemporary events, such as childhood reactions to parental behaviors. As these affective states move toward expression, archetypal energy is activated, resulting in the emergence of images laden with feeling. This, in Jung's terms, is the dynamic responsible for the journeyer's experience of images that are alive with feeling and power.

The emotional flares that help the therapist understand patterns emerging into consciousness can, when guided by reason and reality, manifest our true selves. A psychotherapist alert to these cues becomes guardian of the affective states as they come to expression. Her guardianship, however, goes beyond insight therapy. To foster more than an intellectual grasp of an image as it arises, she may invite it to come to expression through physical activity. Bodywork, artistic renderings, and gestalt release all augment emotional therapeutics, as does journeying.

Symbols

A century ago Freud told us that the unconscious communicates with the conscious mind by means of symbols, many of which appear in dreams and ASC imagery. Jung differentiated between two types: *natural* symbols, which originate within the unconscious and represent basic archetypal motifs, and *cultural* symbols, which portray long-standing societal or religious "truths."[14] Tracing the history of natural symbols to their origins in the oldest primitive societies, Jung concluded that the ancient shamanic images depicted in Eliade's classic text illustrate basic archetypal motifs. Here we have a remarkable nexus: *the symbols that spring from the unconscious connect us to nature and to the natural order of the universe.*

Jung went on to explain that built into the human psyche is a matrix of energy linking us to life-giving, soul-quenching primordial sources. But over time, he said, we disengaged from this matrix to such an extent that we are no longer nourished by the early reservoirs of sustenance. In the pursuit of scientific mastery over matter, humanity has severed its ties to the natural world. Jung wrote:

> Man feels himself isolated in the cosmos. He is no longer involved in nature and has lost his emotional participation in natural events, which hitherto had a symbolic meaning for him. . . . His immedi-

ate communication with nature is gone forever, and the emotional energy it generated has sunk into the unconscious.[15]

Even religions appear to rely more on the spoken word and rational interpretations than on immediate perceptions and symbolic experiences. In Jung's words:

> We are so captivated by and entangled in our subjective consciousness that we have simply forgotten the age-old fact that God speaks chiefly through dreams and visions. The Buddhist discards the world of unconscious fantasies as "distractions" and useless illusions; the Christian puts his Church and his Bible between himself and his unconscious; and the rationalist intellectual does not yet know that his consciousness is not his total psyche, in spite of the fact that for more than seventy years the unconscious has been a basic scientific concept that is indispensable to any serious student of psychology.[16]

The energy of both natural and cultural symbols, whether we access it or not, is woven not only into our psychic makeup but also into the fabric of society. The face of the primitive is paraded through the streets of New Orleans at Mardi Gras time and through Native American pueblos of the Southwest on feast days. When human contact with these vital symbols of the archetypal world is ruptured, their numinosity—that is, the energy ordinarily emitted by them—withdraws into the unconscious. There the energy rallies around such unresolved motifs as prejudice and intolerance, contributing to the decline of moral and spiritual values and the degeneration of cultures. Hidden and unacknowledged, it awaits its release with ever-escalating intensity.

The Shadow

Ignored and repressed energy formulates the shadow self—an entity which, perhaps more than any other, strengthens the grip of violence and fear in our society. "Even tendencies that might be able to exert a beneficial influence turn into veritable demons when they are repressed," said Jung.[17] Tremendous stores of energy are sapped to keep these shadow emotions in check. What's more, they expand as we mature.

From birth onward, the unconscious portion of the psyche accumulates the feeling energy that parental and societal figures were not able to tolerate. And still today, the feelings we fail to recognize as our own and the emotions we refuse to express sink out of sight into unconsciousness, where they become fodder for this shadow self. The false self swells as it feeds on whatever validation it can wrest from the external environment while the true self languishes out of sight.

A society in which individuals are barred from giving authentic expression to their innermost feelings prohibits instinctual, archetypal energy from moving into consciousness. Disconnected, these shadow feelings appear in dreams, or are projected onto others, causing us to attribute to them the qualities we cannot acknowledge in ourselves. Terrorists, for instance, claim to hate the power and control of government, yet emanating from their own psyches are annihilating displays of power and control.

Are the acts of terrorists *evil*, as some social analysts contend? Are we living in a world dominated by violent forces over which we have no control? Jung would say that the so-called evil we see perpetrated is largely the result of repression, which can be prevented. As he put it, "Much of the evil in the world comes from the fact that man in general is hopelessly unconscious, as it is also true that with increasing insight we can combat this evil at its source in ourselves, in the same way that science enables us to deal obviously with injuries inflicted from without."[18] The sad truth is that much of what we experience as evil is material from the shadow self projected onto figures *outside the self.*

The enemy resides within, yet alongside it lies the antidote to our suffering. Psychologists tell us that in meeting the shadow self, we mitigate its intensity by yoking ourselves to our forgotten potentials. Author Connie Zweig and Jungian therapist Jeremiah Abrams say, "When we are in a proper relationship to it, the unconscious is not a demoniacal monster."[19]

From Shadow to Light

Jung's psychological-philosophical terminology helps describe the impact of shamanic phenomena on the psyche. The collective unconscious, as it is birthed from the "dark confines of the earth," erupts into healing expression through shamanic movement. That is, *the spirit world encountered in journeying is none other than the landscape of this collective unconscious illuminated by the release of archetypal energy long bound to its internal matrix.*

Jung lamented the disappearance of expressed archetypal energy, which in earlier civilizations had been culturally sanctioned, if not celebrated. He mourned the loss of interchange between the natural and the supernatural worlds, which created a channel for the movement of energy from the unconscious to physical manifestation. But he also constructed a bridge between the ills that vex humanity and the discarded "source" that alone is able to redeem and redress the attendant losses. By traversing this bridge, we can move from the conscious to the unconscious.

Archetypal reconnection can be accomplished in a number of ways. Among them, active imagination and dreamwork are perhaps the most well-known modalities. The original route, however, is the shamanic path. The psychotherapeutic incorporation of shamanic ideas and images—which Jung cited as "illuminating" examples of natural archetypal motifs—links us with a healing power traceable to our ancient roots.[20]

Historically, shamanic rituals were performed by a shaman to foster community healing. Now we are learning how shamanic activity can be of benefit when utilized for the *individual*—and by the individual. The journeyer, whether she is a shaman acting on behalf of a client or an individual acting on her own behalf, *activates archetypal energy.* In so doing, she accesses a source capable of palliating anguish or distress.

For some individuals, being consistently nurtured and held in reverie by shamanic beings provides a sense of wholeness and connectedness never before experienced. For others, the shamanic arena provides a holding and transforming environment conducive to the articulation of fear, shame, guilt, grief, or anger never before expressed. Whenever we see psychological woundedness surfacing in violent acts, we may rest assured that the containment and transformation of energy available through journeying can offer a potent healing alternative.

Symbols Revisited

The words *image* and *symbol* appear throughout this discussion of alchemical transformation, giving rise to a provocative question: *Are the power animals and spirit helpers we meet in nonordinary reality merely inert images or symbols, or are they imbued with a life of their own?* Shamans and countless fellow journeyers attest to the vitality of these figures, describing encounters with them as "real as every-day life." Jung himself bore witness to their reality in an account of his meeting with a "guru" he called Philemon: "Philemon and other figures of my fantasies brought home to me the crucial insight that there are things in the psyche which I do not produce, but which produce themselves and have their own life. Philemon represented a force which was not myself."[21] Years later, while talking to a friend of Mahatma Gandhi's, Jung found it "illuminating and reassuring" to learn that in India, some individuals have spirits for teachers.[22]

Jung met his spirit guide in the nonordinary reality he called "fantasy." His understanding of symbols as links to the natural order of the universe subsequently penetrated the metaphysical realm. As time passed, Jung moved ever closer to the shamanic world—a realm harboring a source of knowledge undetectable by our organs of perception, and vibrantly dynamic whether or not the soul leaves the body to commune with that source. True to shamanic tradition, Jung's connection with Philemon endured, broadening his grasp of the psyche.

Encounters that occur in journeying are remarkably similar to Jung's. When first instructing clients in ways to meet a power animal or spirit guide, I tell them that they are embarking on a relation-ship much like those of ordinary reality. And it is true; journeyers and power animals communicate on a regular basis—playing together, exchanging gifts, and engaging in many other activities that strengthen their deepening bond. In addition, journeyers approach teachers in the upper world with deference, assuming the role of learners about to become privy to information that will be of great benefit to their lives.

Upper world teachers take on human form and may embody historical, religious, or ancestral figures. A client of mine delightfully discovered one of her teachers to be her revered deceased grandmother. Another client, a woman of Hispanic heritage, receives teachings from a Native American elder. Additional mentors may appear spontaneously in journey, or they may appear when a particular teaching is finished.

The following excerpt describes a beginning relationship between a client named Ann and an upper world teacher.

> I go to my place in the canyon. I float up to the cliff and stand for a moment. Then I float up higher and higher, and come to a mist—a type of very thin membrane—and pop through. I'm standing on a cloud, asking for my teacher. I look all around and see a lot of mist coming off the other clouds. I decide to go higher and ask again for my teacher. I pause at the next level and see a man in brown robes, with a rope tied around his waist, a beard, and a dove on his shoulder. He smiles. He has soft, brown eyes.
>
> I ask if he's my teacher, and he says, "Yes." He sits on a low bench, and I ask if he is St. Francis of Assisi, because that is who he looks like. "Yes," he answers. He says that he has been watching me since I was born and that he has helped me connect with nature—which has been so important in my life.
>
> I tell him about the time I went to the library and tried to learn more about him, something I did seemingly out of the blue. I tell him I am cautious about having a man as a teacher at this point in my life, and he says he understands.
>
> He asks me to sit down. I ask if I could sit against a tree trunk. And even though it is the upper world, we find a tree. I tell him that I don't know much about the upper world or about what grows here, and we both laugh.
>
> He is sitting on the grass opposite me now. I ask if there are flies in heaven, and we laugh again.

This teacher, appearing in the human form of St. Francis, came into Ann's journeying experience as she was undergoing a major shift in her life. In succeeding journeys, his many suggestions for enhancing her connection with nature contributed not only to a more flexible transition period but to a grounded new beginning. She moved to a modest dwelling at the city's edge and left her full-time job for part-time employment that freed her up for the painting she longed to do.

In some respects, Ann's initial encounter with her upper world teacher is reminiscent of student-teacher meetings that take place in ordinary reality. Her words exude a naturalness, to the point of expressing her concern about having a male teacher. Her sense of humor sparks laughter. And she muses over her earlier attempt to learn about this saint—a phenomenon that falls under the rubric of synchronicity, or according to Jung, coincidental occurrences attributed not to chance but to an archetype manifesting in both physical and mental realms.[23]

Actually, the alliances forged between journeyers and their spirit helpers go well *beyond* those formed in ordinary reality. Shamanic beings offer a stability, loyalty, acceptance, and wisdom we humans can only partially provide. They also invite us to participate in wholesome interrelating. To begin with, they give us their dedicated presence. No matter what behaviors we may exhibit in ordinary reality, no matter what moods we may display in journey, the spirit helpers listen, guide, and heal. We may not always like the counsel they offer, but commitment to our welfare so flavors their activity that it is almost impossible not to seriously consider their advice. Curiously enough, even the exasperation we express in response to such unwanted counsel is greeted with acceptance. In the end, whether we implement the journey suggestions or disregard them, the power animals and teachers sustain their allegiance to us, free of judgment and penalty. Out of this unconditional acceptance arises trust.

Over time, experiences of this sort shift our perception of *ordinary* reality. The shamanic beings' empathic witnessing of our dilemmas as well as their compassionate healing responses model an open-hearted objectivity that we, too, can strive for. A power animal's ability to remain firm despite our requests that he change his approach shows us that we can remain true to ourselves while allowing others to remain true to themselves. From spirit helpers we glean a new understanding of "being in relationship," and as if by osmosis, we may slowly acquire the ability to interact with others the way journey beings interact with us.

Initially, we journey in response to a source of healing that appears to beckon from outside ourselves. We connect to this source not through the aid of some guru or cleric, but rather under the power of our own intent. Upon our arrival, we find a spiritual democracy in which no hierarchy reigns and each individual's path resonates with his own temperament and style of expression. Here we receive healing information, cross the bridge to our inner selves, forge relationships with lost parts of our souls, and transform fragmentation into wholeness. As we return to ordinary reality, we bring forth our unity, and in so doing we augment the whole of society.

The Meeting Place

The shaman and the psychologist enter the same dream. In this shared dream she sleeps under the tree while he is guided to a multilevel structure. Stepping inside, he heads for the basement where he finds—amid many books and a great deal of sophisticated technology—a little girl clutching the mane of a lion. He recognizes the child as a "piece" of his dreaming companion lost in the world of words and machines. He brings the girl and the large cat back to the tree, blowing them into the woman's heart. In the dream she wakes up filled with hope and excitement, not knowing exactly why. Seeing her fellow dreamer next to her, she greets him, and together they walk to the building. They enter a room on the main level and sit before a screen that lights up as the psychologist places a wire on the shaman's forehead. Colored tracings appear on the screen, registering his state of consciousness. He gazes in wonderment at the strange fixture.

THE OLDEST KNOWN CATALYST FOR HEALING RISES FROM THE DEPTHS OF the psyche, igniting creative impulses from the part of the self once considered solely instinctual. We have seen how this energy brings its curative touch to woundedness. We have also seen that when the woundedness is developmental, it relies on the ripening of the true self for restoration. By what means does an adult continue fulfilling his early needs for connection and separation? How do psychologists *account for* this movement toward the completion of unresolved tasks of childhood?

While child development investigators have unearthed impressive findings in recent years, researchers in adult development have not been idle; many have presented evidence on how we humans mature through the stages of life. Among them is psychiatrist George Vaillant, who reminds us of our inherent resiliency— a capacity for psychological growth that continues into adulthood. He associates this potential with "the internalization of a holding environment" that occurs as the self matures, describing in scholarly terms—and perhaps without even knowing it—the precise role of the power animals in their interactions with journeyers.[1] Other psychological changes that accompany adult development also sound oddly similar to the dynamics of journeying.

These recent findings appear to be leading psychology toward an intersection with the earliest healing tradition known to humanity. Already we can envision at the meeting place a synergy offering great promise for mending our developmental gaps, and much more as well.

The Tasks of the Ego

We have spoken of the self, but what of the ego? Has it become a disenfranchised stepchild of development? Where does it fit in today's psychological landscape?

The Ego and the Self
Originally, Freud's term *das ich* (the ego) had two meanings—the experiencing self and a psychic organizing structure, the latter of which dominated early psychoanalytic thought. Most Freudians presented this ego structure as a mediator between the instinctual

energy of the id and the dictates of the superego, or conscience, and also as the organizing principle of the psyche that enables us to perceive, reason, solve problems, and interact with the external world. Over time, the idea of the self, with its subjective experiences and creativity, rejoined the concept of ego, generating terms such as "executive self," "sense of self," and "sense of identity."[2] For Daniel Stern, who focuses on subjective interactions of the infant, the *core self* is the organizer of development.

Today, in some quarters, the word *ego* is considered tainted. A person's ego, we say, is "too big" or "always getting in the way." Some spiritual traditions advocate its diminishment, or even its dissolution. The fact is this seat of intelligence and rationality so essential to human survival is suffering a bad rap because its development has often been hindered—the effects of which sooner or later become apparent. For example, an individual may lack a capacity for realistic thinking; exhibit flighty or impulsive behavior; undergo a splitting of the personality; be easily enraged; or have a narcissistic need for constant attention, otherwise known as an "insatiable ego." With this in mind, ego *transcendence* makes more sense than ego abdication. Yet, to transcend it, we must have in place a mature and adequately functioning ego.

A mature and functioning ego, as Freud suggested, is composed not only of the whole experiencing self but of the organizing mental structure as well. Hence, to overcome our contemporary dilemma, we might think of the self emerging from the behind-the-scenes activities of an organizing structure.

The Maturing Ego

Healthy infant development, as we have seen, calls for both the internalization of supportive, nurturing figures and the establishment of an independent sense of self. All the while, unacceptable impulses and wishes push forth from the unconscious and demands to conform press inward from the environment. In early childhood and on into adulthood, the organizing structure of the ego helps us cope with these stressors by calling on defense mechanisms that distort inner and outer realities to protect us from anxiety, guilt, and unacceptable impulses. Finding anger unaccept-able, for example, a child will use *repression* to quell his rage at an abusing parent, and thereby avoid subjecting himself to disap-proval or further harm. After an upsetting day at work, a woman will resort to *displacement*, yelling at her husband rather than her boss, and thereby protecting her job security.

These and all other ego defenses operate unconsciously and dis-tort reality to varying degrees. According to Vaillant, delusions of persecution, at one end of the continuum, constitute a "psychotic" style of defense, while delayed gratification, at the other, repre-sents a "mature" defense.[3]

Vaillant, upon investigating data from three studies that tracked more than 2,200 individuals over a fifty- to seventy-year period, found the *most mature ego defenses* among individuals who had attained the *highest degrees of psychological adjustment.* A secure sense of self, he noted, goes hand in hand with not taking oneself too seri-ously; being able to sublimate energy into creative endeavors; plan-ning for the future; an ability to resolve conflicts through the post-ponement of gratification or an appropriate downplaying or rechanneling of impulses; and involvement in altruistic activities.[4]

Defenses work on our behalf, altering reality by creatively rear-ranging conflicts into more manageable situations. The resulting distortions give us time to acclimate to life's contingencies until the anxiety of the threatening situation can be borne. Imagine the par-ents of a child with a terminal illness who, unable to accept the impli-cation of the diagnosis, visit clinic after clinic until their defenses are worn so thin that they can at last hear the unfortunate truth. This period of *denial* may be just what they needed, not only to gather strength for the difficult days ahead but also to provide an atmos-phere of possibility for the failing child. After their child's death, these parents may engage in *altruistic* endeavors—volunteering time and energy to other suffering children, doing for them what they wanted others to do for their child.

Here is another example of the ego's defenses at work. Jane, a woman I know, solicited a friend's support for her reluctance to pursue long-fantasized tennis lessons, *intellectualizing* about her lack of motivation, money, and time, rather than confronting her fear of failure. Later she *sublimated* her athletic aspirations by writing vignettes about Olympic hopefuls. Then one day she ventured a glimpse at her fear and cautiously enrolled in a beginning tennis class.

The Alchemy of the Ego

Wherever a particular defense mechanism happens to fall on the continuum of adaptiveness, its purpose is to activate the psychological immune system's capacity for resiliency. Bending and springing back without breaking allows us to overcome disadvantage. The prime mover here is the innate wisdom of the ego, as it learns to "spin straw into gold." Through this "alchemy of the ego," Vaillant tells us, the distorting tendencies of the defense mechanisms lead us toward integration and away from insanity.[5] So we see that the alchemical process of growth that transmutes ordinary materials into something of merit is as plausible to Vaillant as it is to Jung. The pinnacle of it all is the ability to tolerate opposing viewpoints, to sustain paradox—a distinguishing feature of ego maturity, or in Jung's terms, individuation.

Ongoing ego maturation, according to Vaillant, is accomplished by "taking people inside," by letting the ego become imprinted with "beloved people and their virtues and their prohibitions,"[6] much as an infant takes in her impression of an emotionally responsive caregiver. As suggested in chapter 3, such a phenomenon stimulates the growth of new neural pathways in the infant's brain; its impact on the adult brain, meanwhile, remains speculative. Someday, brain imaging will no doubt elucidate what happens neurobiologically in moments of emotional imprinting for infants *and* adults. At that point, we will learn if theory and research have brought us as close to the mark as experts suggest they have.

The same "taking in" that occurs during ego maturation occurs in journeying as the individual internalizes journey beings. Internalizing, like imprinting, depends not only on the acceptance or support of loved ones but also on temperamental fit: the power animal who comes forward in response to our call resonates with our personality, needs, and deficits. The later arrival of additional power animals brings the energies needed for new tasks. A person whose nurturing power animal is a deer, for example, may find the deer joined by a male lion when she detects a need for more assertiveness.

Spirituality and the Ego

Longitudinal data, which help researchers identify significant trends and influences over time, enabled Vaillant to observe a connection between ego maturation, creativity, and a sense of "religious wonder."[7] The thread of spirituality weaving through the lives of many of his subjects (and, I suspect, countless "nonsubjects"), he hypothesizes, has been energized by dreams, sacred places, play (including ritual), and the integration of idea and affect.

Dreams move us beyond all that is immediately perceptible. The dreaming we do while awake is as important as that which we do while asleep, because imagination fosters maturation of the defenses as well as faith. While daydreaming, we replay the past and prepare for the future, entertaining possibilities, practicing new options, and trying out new directions. Journeying offers similar opportunities: awake and in an altered state of consciousness, we transcend the present, engaging in activities with shamanic beings, sharing in their power, and stretching beyond preconceived notions of our abilities.

Sacred places, like the painted caves at Lascaux in southwestern France or historic cathedrals throughout Europe, foster experiences reminiscent of a holding environment. In such spaces we are reminded of the promise of connection and the value of purpose in our lives. Earthly caverns ignited the creativity of Paleolithic artists whose drawings, still electric with energy, engender awe. Individuals today describe journey sites—both the points of embarkation and the interior settings—in sacred terms, commenting, "I feel a sense of reverence here," "This is a holy place," or "Blessings come to me while I sit in the meadow with my power animal." Circles of healing, rushing rivers, and pristine mountains exude mystery while wrapping us in an envelope of protection.

Play—an activity too often interrupted in childhood—gives voice to inner essence and promotes the prospering of the true self. Play creates order out of disorder, bringing to the environment something that was not there before. Journeying grants us this experience as well, through capricious, spontaneous interactions with the power animals. Ritual, too, shapes play into reality, bringing forth new psychological patterns while stripping away old ones. According to Vaillant, it even invigorates the infusion of a new identity: "[The ritualistic dance] is a mystic unity. The one has *become* the other. In his magic dance, the Aboriginal dancer *is* a kangaroo."[8] In the shamanic world, when one meets a new power animal, he is advised to dance its essence. How often psychological theorists think in shamanic terms without knowing it!

The integration of idea and affect occurs as we become aware of feeling states, realistically assess the environment, and choose new growth-promoting behaviors, all of which deepen our faith in the order and unity of life. Thinking and feeling are not mutually exclusive. The anger I feel when someone misleads me can coexist with my decision to mediate with the person. Rather than lash out in a voracious diatribe, I can channel my anger into negotiation—and hence put a new spin on my approach to adversarial relationships. Journeying, likewise, offers limitless opportunities for organizing thoughts and feelings. I may initiate a journey to examine feelings of discouragement about the fragmentation of an important relationship. Acknowledging my feelings, the shamanic beings may illuminate ideas for reconciliation.

Ego maturity unfolds with life experience. The more impressions of nurturing figures we assimilate and the more we pursue our individuation, the more our ego defenses mature, enabling us to more genuinely connect with others while remaining true to ourselves. Many individuals hampered by environmental deficiencies and temperamental challenges, however, struggle along this developmental incline. The good news is that by furnishing opportunities to internalize shamanic beings, journeying is able to inject a power boost into these arduous quests for ego maturity.

With ego maturity, we acquire a clear sense of self. Knowing where the self ends and the "other" begins, we replace projection with empathy. When the self is contained and secure in its worth, we as individuals, far from being self-invested, accord the same respect to others as we do to ourselves. When the altruism of "doing for others" is not motivated by a desire for return or secondary gain, who knows—we may well have arrived at ego transcendence.

The Emotions Accompanying Change

In his book *Human Change Process*, psychologist Michael Mahoney states:

> We are leaning that psychological change is neither simple nor easy and yet that it is pervasive and relentless. . . . Of central importance to psychotherapy practitioners is the realization that the processes underlying human psychological change are nonlinear and complex, thereby preventing perfect predictions of what will happen to the particulars of any given individual's life.[9]

Mahoney backs up these words with a comprehensive review of the literature, offering mounting evidence that psychological change continues throughout life. His survey also tells us that human change is accompanied by emotion, which plays a central role in the depth and breadth of the alterations.[10] So it appears that the formative years mark only the beginning of a lifelong relationship between affect and adjustment.

The Emotion-Change Equation in Psychotherapy

The interaction between emotion and change is intrinsic to psychotherapy: individuals seek out a therapist because they are distressed, additional feelings arise in the therapeutic dialogue, and the ensuing changes generate new emotional reactions. Endorsing the importance of feelings, psychoanalyst Franz Alexander told us decades ago that insights alone cannot trigger adjustment; for change to occur, he said, a "corrective emotional experience" is necessary.[11] Psychologists Leslie Greenberg and Jeremy Safran have gone one step further by suggesting that nonverbal methods of emotional stimulation such as imagery, enactments, and the use of music and drawing promote therapeutic change more effectively than do strictly verbal interactions.[12]

The emotion-change equation rests firmly in the hands of the facilitating psychotherapist. Researchers tell us that of all the variables affecting client change and therapy outcome, the emotional quality of the therapeutic relationship is second only to the client's background and the motivational influences she brings to therapy.[13, 14] Change, it turns out, hinges less on applying techniques than on being with the client's experiences and feelings. Responding to shades of emotion, innuendoes of yearning, and sparks of possibility inspires collaborative effort, creating an alliance capable of initiating change.

To be an effective container, must the therapist be a "wounded healer," as some commentators have suggested? In response to this question, two schools of thought have arisen. One insists that personal suffering strengthens a practitioner's healing ability, while the other points out that a psychotherapist's unresolved pain and dysfunction will interfere with his responsible and ethical treatment of clients. Research to date has not provided a definitive answer.

For clarification we must look elsewhere. History abounds with healing figures who have undergone rigorous challenges to their physical and psychological well-being. Shamans are illustrious in this respect. Milton Erickson, founder of an innovative style of curative hypnosis, was dyslexic and twice paralyzed by polio. Studies in human change have led Mahoney to this conclusion: "The question is of course, complex. The psychotherapist who has never struggled with intense feelings of vulnerability or existential predicaments may have difficulty understanding (let alone feeling empathic toward) a client for whom these are overwhelming concerns."[15]

Common sense tells us that a psychotherapist who is uncomfortable with emotional intensity will impede therapeutic progress. It also stands to reason that unless a psychotherapist has experienced the emotional turmoil inherent in the struggle for a grounded and healthy sense of self—whether this experience has come in the natural, integrative course of development or in later reparative efforts—his capacity to contain and midwife a client's change-shaping emotions will be compromised.

In the final analysis, whether or not a psychotherapist considers himself wounded, he is obligated to be aware of his own emotional resistance to client affect, and to seek guidance in sorting out his uncomfortable reactions. Healing is a process, and the healer who ongoingly walks a path committed to self-healing shows both a resilient and a realistic bent.

The Emotion-Change Relationship in Shamanic Psychotherapeutics

Therapists who integrate shamanic techniques into their psychotherapeutic practice help further the alchemical sparks of change. Why? Because in journeying, emotion occurs naturally and spontaneously. By contrast, in reporting dreams clients may view their content as observers, unmoved by feelings or reactions. They may even discount dream activity that seems too foreign to relate to. Journeys, on the other hand, are most often subjective, and sometimes teeming with emotion. While in the presence of journeying clients, I have seen hands gesturing and feet moving rhythmically, and have heard the singing of songs and watched the spilling of tears. Emotion accompanies the journey experience, enkindling it into the mysterious and powerful endeavor that it is. All the while, the archetype is moving into expression, either slowly and gently, or with great vigor.

Shamanism brings to the psychological domain a force that is both natural and spiritual— natural, because it is rooted in nature and in humankind's earliest relationships with the elements, and spiritual, because it illuminates the client's relationship with her soul. This approach does not transport a person to other realms for purposes of a magical experience; rather, it facilitates a healing of the body and soul through the doorway of the mind that knows how to expand into spirit. The energy of shamanism rises from the folds of the earth (via the power animals and spirit helpers) and ignites with the energy showering down from above (via the spiritual teachers). The drumming, like the beat of the heart, announces the life of spirit and invites entry into a place where the sacred meets the profane, where shamanic strength knows human weakness and wisdom casts its light on shadow emotions.

The journey's wisdom is perfectly matched to the needs and anguish of the journeyer. It nourishes her like a knowing grandmother gazes upon her newly born grandchild, soothes her tears in infancy, and stands by at arm's length during her tantrums in toddlerhood, aware that these, too, lead to adjustment in the world.

Within the container of the wisdom-infused journey, the energy of emotion is transmuted. Any resulting anger is not released onto a random or even select group of violators, bringing woe unto them. Rather, the projection of unacceptable impulses, the blaming of others for personal faults and failures, is held within the journey, where it is alchemically transformed into something of greater merit. The energy released in this experience leaves the journeyer cleansed and further healed.

Those who use journeying as a vehicle for change do so with a variety of intents. Some seek to expand their creativity; others hope to overcome their passivity. Some set out to release repressed anger; others look for bounded and appropriate ways of expressing their anger. In each instance, the therapist assists by containing the accompanying emotion.

In the end it is the client's active participation in the change that makes all the difference—a valuable consideration amid today's increasing scrutiny of healer-healee relationships. Clients want to make informed choices by using both the knowledge of experts and the knowledge contained in their own minds and bodies. It is gratifying to tap into our own healing resources; it is empowering to discover that healing can occur as a result of a self-generated process, and not solely because of something a therapist did or said. Shamanic Psychotherapeutics fulfills all these imperatives, and what's more, it lessens the authoritarian role of the therapist, diminishes transference and countertransference, and enhances the client's appreciation of *herself* as a healer.

Global Healing

It is time to begin promulgating an awareness of shamanic healing principles. Why? Because never before has a global community been more evident, and the mental health of its members more precarious. Foresighted psychotherapists are sensing a burning need to share information across interdenominational healing lines. At the same time, individuals from all walks of life are crying out with ecumenical urgency for ever more potent modes of healing.

We now know that learning can alter aggressive behavior patterns, and yet feelings of helplessness and hopelessness are running rampant. Escalating forces of destruction are dismantling aspirations and opportunities for change. Individuals are becoming immobilized, trapped in the belief that isolated personal efforts to effect change cannot possibly impact on the greater chaos. Inert are the impulses that might otherwise lead to constructive activity.

Perhaps the greatest contributor to this paralysis is the collective unconscious—the portion of the psyche that houses the accumulated experiences of all preceding generations. Just as we are consciously connected to one another by telecommunications networks capable of establishing immediate linkage from one end of the globe to another, on an unconscious level we are connected by universal imprints of behavior, emotional responsiveness, and potentiality. Moreover, each time the demonstration of any of these potentialities falters or fails, its energy ferments and the gathering intensity is transmitted across a web of unconsciousness to the rest of humanity, casting an enormous shadow.

This collective shadow, composed of the consolidated rejections of social groups projected outward onto others, divides the world into black and white, "us and them," the valued and the devalued. Repudiation, scapegoating, racism, and dogmatism are all signs of the collective shadow at work. Groups indulging in acts of racial supremacy or religious righteousness are more often than not reenacting the violations of their abusers. Entire wars are waged in defense of "sacred beliefs"—that is, in opposition to atrocities perpetrated by *others* who have placed themselves in positions of moral superiority.

The individual shadow finds patronage in the collective darkness. There it discovers safety in numbers and an opportunity to align with other shadows in projecting buried feelings onto political or institutional figures or philosophies. Terrorists and anarchists, the Hitlers and the Husseins, all serve as collective repositories for the darkness we cannot recognize in ourselves. At a certain point, when the projections cast upon an individual or organization reach a critical mass, they erupt. Said another way, an angry teenager wielding a gun is empowered by our collective investment in refusing to acknowledge the hatred dwelling in our own unconscious.

The recourse we have to the violence in our midst is to behold the shadow within us. In the introduction to a series of essays on the shadow, Connie Zweig and Jeremiah Abrams write:

> The aim of meeting the shadow is to develop an ongoing relationship with it, to expand our sense of self by balancing the one-sidedness of our conscious attitudes with our unconscious depths. . . . Perhaps we can also, in this way, refrain from adding our personal darkness to the destiny of the collective shadow.[16]

Poet-philosopher Robert Bly puts it this way: "People who are passive toward their projected material contribute to the danger of nuclear war, because every bit of energy that we don't actively engage with language or art is floating somewhere in the air above. . . ."[17]

Having encountered our shadow self, how do we establish a "relationship" with it, and what can we do with this projected material? In our sobering acknowledgment of shadow emotions, we connect with them; honoring them as our own we can then, one by one, "take back" our projections. In fact, the more of this energy we manage to reclaim, the more we reduce the mass of the collective shadow and the pressure that forces others to release destructive energy.

Not only are we individually capable of siphoning off pressure from the collective unconscious by digesting material from the personal shadow; but by activating archetypal material, we may also be able to propel an alchemical spark through the invisible network of collective consciousness, invigorating psychic expansion and growth. As the archetypal energies of sublimation, altruism, suppression, anticipation, humor, and empathy come forward, they reflect a life lived through individual expression rather than collective repression. Spreading across the collective web, these energies catalyze movement toward individuation. From this perspective, the archetypal ripening of any individual would invigorate the healing of the whole of humanity. And it would defuse the powerlessness felt by people who see no means for impeding the escalation of chaos and violence in the world. Admitting to emotions that have been denied and defended against is the work of heroes and heroines, and at once an act of self-empathy and collective compassion.

Humanity's greatest challenge is to raise to conscious awareness the existential paradox that enfolds us. Jung spelled it out in these terms:

> There is no light without shadow and no psychic wholeness without imperfection. To round itself out, life calls not for perfection but for completeness; and for this the "thorn in the flesh" is needed, the suffering of defects without which there is no progress and no ascent.[18]

The human shadow casts its silhouette vertically and horizontally. Vertically, it pushes and pulls at the individual psyche, begging for expression; horizontally, it accumulates in the pool of the collective psyche. This situation poses a major dilemma: as we individually and collectively strive for what is valued as good, the energy causing the "undoing" of good lurks outside our awareness. In other words, attempts directed toward the noble are undermined by the pull of selfish concerns. As Jungian analyst Jolande Jacobi writes:

A swing toward one side is always followed by an equal swing toward the other. Peace is found *only at the center,* where man can be wholly man, neither angel nor devil, but simply man, partaker of both worlds. . . . This center is also the place where the Divine filters through into the soul and reveals itself in the God-images, in the Self.[19]

Jacobi calls this center a state of balance—"a state in which both worlds, the light and the dark, the good and the bad, the joyful and the sorrowful, are united in self-evident acceptance and reflect the true nature of man, his inborn duality."[20] It is where the process of change alchemically transforms the energy of opposites into a unity of acceptance and wisdom. It is also where Jacobi says we find God.

Countless religions and philosophies address the spiritual interconnectedness of humankind. Christians tell us the mystical body of Christ reflects a communion of human souls. Teilhard de Chardin, a paleontologist and French Jesuit priest, has coined the term "noogenesis" to describe the "concentration and collective march forward of human thought."[21] Whether the link to spirit is formalized through religion or actualized through a belief in an animating principle, it is the factor most in need of attention in today's troubled world, including the world of psychology.

As violence sits at our doorstep and the threat of extinction resounds in our ears, we can turn to journeying for a pathway of communication with the soul. Guided to the lower world and the upper world, we will not only watch but actually animate the unfolding of an exquisite story featuring ourselves and the gods of our being. The focus of our attention will be not myth—the body of legendary stories used to explain archetypal phenomena—but *activation of archetypal energy* through direct participation. Returning to ordinary reality, we will then be able to say with certainty that journeying provides an experience of one's own being, free of all filters, including the analyst's interpretations, myth's elucidations, and theory's postulations. And we will know that the healing balm for our internal fractures is the self communing with the universal.

The movement of energy that occurs while journeying and the affective response to archetypal actualizations enliven us and connect us with our truest source. In its best expression this flow of psychic energy from the unconscious enhances the community, promotes constructive enterprise, and brings unity to human purpose. We leave the "me generations" behind as the maturing ego, grounded in a resilient selfhood, sponsors individual contributions to a dynamic and creative social milieu.

That Fruit Be Brought to Bear

Shamans search for lost pieces of soul and return them to members of their community. Psychologists investigate the workings of the mind and strive to validate their methodological approaches. The meeting of shamanic spirit and psychological mind animates the heart of holism. This heart, beating to an unbroken rhythm, unites with the cadence of humanity's call. We, in turn, dance to the synergy of new healing pulses.

What might the future hold for these healing arts? Certainly the two disciplines are distinct; the core of the shamanic apple cannot be grafted into the psychological orange, and it is incredulous to think of the shamanic apple striving for specialized segmentation. At the same time, each has something important to offer the other.

Shamanism has soul to give to psychology. The small second fruit on that navel orange, already seeded by psychologist-spiritualists, has the potential to blossom, since it is infused with the spirit of a tradition that illumines, animates, and restores the psyche of humankind. This breath of vital essence may come either from the segments of psychology that allow for soul or from individual psychologists scattered throughout the ranks. Incorporated into the psychological arena, shamanic principles can holistically enhance both scientism and humanism.

Psychology has science to give to shamanism. With an empirical base, this amphitheater of healing will be sufficiently fortified to extend its validity and appeal to a broader spectrum of individuals poised on the cusp of twenty-first-century thinking. The shamanic journey, an expanded use of altered states of consciousness, is as capable of being empirically evaluated as any other ASC. Subjected to such brain imaging techniques as PET (positron emission tomography) and FMRI (functional magnetic resonance imaging), it is likely to yield a wealth of information about its impact on cogitating, feeling, and remembering. Indeed, investigations of shamanic phenomena have already begun, prompted primarily by The Foundation for Shamanic Studies. As research continues, the assessments are sure to be heuristically invaluable. I, for one, am excited by the possibility of tracking brain activity during the journey experience.

Across eons of time, the shamanic imprint has deepened, waiting for humanity to penetrate its wisdom. And now "soulful" psychotherapy beckons. It calls to clients bewildered by the polarity of their nature. It summons psychotherapists who, supported by an understanding of human resiliency and the maturing self, are determined to guide their charges to a place of balance where they will no longer be at the mercy of opposing forces. At this soulful center, warmed and anchored by the alchemical matrix of the shamanic journey, the angst of the world can be contained and transformed.

Notes

Prologue

1. Michael Balint, *The Basic Fault: Therapeutic Aspects of Regression* (London: Tavistock, 1968), p. 22.

2. Sandra Ingerman, *Soul Retrieval: Mending the Fragmented Self* (San Francisco: Harper, 1991).

3. Ibid.

4. John Bradshaw, *Relationships*. An audiotape produced by Bradshaw Cassettes, 1986.

5. Harville Hendrix, *Getting the Love You Want: A Guide for Couples* (New York: Henry Holt, 1988), pp. 227–228. The container exercise referred to begins with an agreement that there be no verbal assault on the character of the spouse and no physical attack on his or her person or property.

Chapter 1

1. Mircea Eliade, *Shamanism: Archaic Techniques of Ecstasy,* trans. by W. R. Trask, Bollingen Series LXXVI (Princeton, NJ: Princeton University Press, 1964), p. 4.

2. Michael Harner, *The Way of the Shaman: A Guide to Power and Healing* (San Francisco: Harper & Row, 1980), p. 20.

3. See Note 1, p. 8.

4. *Longman Dictionary of Psychology and Psychiatry,* s.v. "psyche."

5. See Note 1, p. 481.

6. Paul G. Bahn and Jean Vertut, *Images of the Ice Age* (London, England: Windward, 1988).

7. "Passions Run High over French Cave Art," *New Scientist* (4 May 1996): 8.

8. Jean-Marie Chauvet, Éliette Brunel Deschamps, and Christian Hillaire, *La Grotte Chauvet* (Paris, France: Editions du Seuil, 1995).

9. See Note 1, p. 220.

10. Roger N. Walsh, *The Spirit of Shamanism* (New York: G. P. Putnam, 1990).

11. See Note 1, p. 507.

12. Åke Hultkrantz, "Shamanism: A Religious Phenomenon?" In

Shaman's Path: Healing, Personal Growth, and Empowerment, ed. by Gary Doore (Boston: Shambhala, 1988), p. 39.

13. Mihály Hoppál, "Shamanism: An Archaic and/or Recent Belief System." In *Shamanism: An Expanded View of Reality*, comp. by Shirley Nicholson (Wheaton, IL: The Theosophical Publishing House, 1987), p. 95.

14. John Lash, *The Seeker's Handbook* (New York: Crown, 1990), p. 371.

15. See Note 1, p. 299.

16. See Note 10, pp. 8–17.

17. See Note 1, pp. 13–66.

18. See Note 1, p. 88.

19. See Note 1, pp. 23–32.

20. See Note 10, ch. 7, p. 81.

21. See Note 1, p. 43.

22. See Note 10, pp. 87–88.

23. See Note 1, pp. 508–509.

24. B. R. Hergenhahn, *An Introduction to the History of Psychology*, 2nd ed. (Belmont, CA: Wadsworth, 1992).

25. James F. Brennan, *History and Systems of Psychology*, 3rd ed. (Englewood Cliffs, NJ: Prentice-Hall, 1990).

26. Daniel N. Robinson, *An Intellectual History of Psychology*, rev. ed. (Madison, WI: The University of Wisconsin Press, 1986).

27. Morton Hunt, *The Story of Psychology* (New York: Doubleday, 1993), p. 309.

28. See Note 24, p. 455.

29. Bruno Bettelheim, *Freud and Man's Soul* (New York: Alfred A. Knopf, 1982).

30. Calvin S. Hall and Gardner Lindzey, *Theories of Personality*, 3rd ed. (New York: John Wiley & Sons, 1978), p. 148.

31. See Note 24, ch. 17.

32. Jan Christian Smuts, *Holism and Evolution* (New York: Viking Press, 1926).

33. Abraham H. Maslow, *Toward a Psychology of Being*, 2nd ed. (New York: D. Van Nostrand, 1968), pp. 87–88.

34. See Note 32, p. 318.

35. D. H. Lajoie, S. I. Shapiro, and T. B. Roberts, "A Historical Analysis of the Statement of Purpose," *The Journal of Transpersonal Psychology* 23, no. 2 (1991): 175–182.

36. Roger Walsh, "The Search for Synthesis: Transpersonal Psychology and the Meeting of East and West, Psychology and Religion, Personal and Transpersonal," *Journal of Humanistic Psychology* 32, no. 1 (1992): 19–45.

37. Miles A. Vich, "The Origins and Growth of Transpersonal Psychology," *Journal of Humanistic Psychology* 30, no. 2 (Spring 1990): 47–50.

38. For a survey demonstrating the existence of two cultures in psychology—one scientific, and the other humanistic—see Gregory A. Kimble, "Psychology's Two Cultures," *American Psychologist* 39, no. 8 (August 1984): 833–839.

39. See Note 26, p. 294.

40. See Note 27, ch 17.

41. Francine Shapiro, *Eye Movement Desensitization and Reprocessing: Basic Principles, Protocols, and Procedures* (New York: The Guilford Press, 1995).

42. *A New Perspective on Reality,* Special Updated Issue of the *Brain/Mind Bulletin.* In *The Holographic Paradigm and Other Paradoxes: Exploring the Leading Edge of* Science, ed. by Ken Wilbur (Boulder & London: Shambhala, 1982), pp. 5–6.

43. John Horgan, "Can Science Explain Consciousness?" *Scientific American* (July 1994): 88–94.

44. See Note 35, p. 178.

45. See Note 25, p. 325.

46. See Note 26, p. 459.

47. See Note 24, p. 557.

48. See Note 33, pp. 81–82, 94.

Chapter 2

1. Jerome D. Frank and Julia B. Frank, *Persuasion and Healing: A Comparative Study of Psychotherapy,* 3rd ed. (Baltimore, MD: The John Hopkins University Press, 1991).

2. Raymond Prince, "Variations in Psychotherapeutic Procedures," *Handbook of Cross-Cultural Psychology: Psychopathology,* vol. 6, ed. by H. C. Triandis and J. G. Draguns (Boston: Allyn and Bacon, 1980), pp. 291–349.

3. See Note 1.

4. See Note 2, p. 297.

5. Michael Harner, *The Way of the Shaman: A Guide to Power and Healing* (San Francisco: Harper & Row, 1980), p. 21.

6. Charles T. Tart, *States of Consciousness* (New York: Dutton, 1975), p. 208.

7. Herbert Benson, *The Relaxation Response* (New York: Avon, 1975).

8. Alfred M. Ludwig, "Altered States of Consciousness." In *Altered States of Consciousness*, 2nd ed., ed. by Charles T. Tart (New York: Anchor Books, 1971).

9. Milton H. Erickson, "Hypnotic Investigation of Psychodynamic Processes." In *The Collected Papers of Milton H. Erickson on Hypnosis*, vol. III, ed. by Ernest L. Rossi (New York: Irvington, 1980), p. 21.

10. See Note 8, pp. 12–24.

11. Ibid, pp. 20–21.

12. Helen Graham, *Mental Imagery in Health Care: An Introduction to Therapeutic Practice* (New York: Chapman & Hall, 1995).

13. Jeanne Achterberg, *Imagery in Healing: Shamanism and Modern Medicine* (Boston: Shambhala, 1985).

14. Rothlyn P. Zahourek, "Imagery." In *Relaxation and Imagery: Tools for Therapeutic Communication and Intervention*, ed. by Rothlyn P. Zahourek (Philadelphia: W. B. Saunders, 1988).

15. O. Carl Simonton, Stephanie Matthews-Simonton, and James Creighton, *Getting Well Again* (Los Angeles: J. P. Tarcher, 1978).

16. See Note 13, p. 6.

17. Ibid., p. 76.

18. See Note 14, pp. 53–83.

19. See Note 12, pp. 2–4.

20. Andrew Weil, *Spontaneous Healing* (New York: Alfred A. Knopf, 1995), p. 71.

21. Ibid., p. 201.

22. S. A. Wilson, L. A. Becker, and R. H. Tinker, "Eye Movement Desensitization and Reprocessing (EMDR) Treatment for Psychologically Traumatized Individuals," *Journal of Consulting and Clinical Psychology* 63, no. 6 (1995): 928–937.

23. Shane M. Murphy, "Models of Imagery in Sport Psychology: A Review," *Journal of Mental Imagery* 14, nos. 3 & 4 (1990): 153–172.

24. Dan Smith, "Imagery in Sport: An Historical and Current Review." In *Mental Imagery*, ed. by Robert G. Kunzendorf (New York: Plenum Press, 1990), pp. 215–224.

25. G. Grouios, H. Kouthouris, and K. Bagiatis, "The Effects of Physical Practice, Mental Practice, and Video—Demonstration Practice on the

Learning of Skiing Skills," *International Journal of Physical Education* 30, no.3 (1993): 25–28.

26. See Note 13, pp. 108–111.

27. Marty Sapp, "The Effects of Guided Imagery on Reducing the Worry and Emotionality Components of Test Anxiety," *Journal of Mental Imagery*, nos. 3 & 4 (1994): 165–180.

28. K. David Shultz, "Imagery and the Control of Depression." In *The Power of Human Imagination: New Methods in Psychotherapy*, ed. by Jerome L. Singer and Kenneth S. Pope (New York: Plenum Press, 1978), pp. 281–307.

29. I. L. Abraham, M. N. Neundorfer, and E. A. Terris, "Effects of Focused Visual Imagery on Cognition and Depression among Nursing Home Residents," *Journal of Mental Imagery* 17, nos. 3 & 4 (1993): 61–76.

30. Barbara Hannah, *Encounters with the Soul: Active Imagination As Developed by C. G. Jung* (Santa Monica, CA: Sigo Press, 1981).

31. Hanscarl Leuner, "Guided Affective Imagery (GAI)," *American Journal of Psychotherapy* 23 (1969): 21.

32. Martha Crampton, "The Use of Mental Imagery in Psychosynthesis," *Journal of Humanistic Psychology* 9 (1969): 140–141.

33. This journey was compiled from the introductory journeys of several clients with whom I have worked.

34. C. G. Jung, *The Structure and Dynamics of the Psyche*, trans. by R. F. C. Hull. In *The Collected Works* 8, 2nd ed., Bollingen Series XX (Princeton, NJ: Princeton University Press, 1969).

35. C. G. Jung, *Symbols of Transformation*, trans. by R. F. C. Hull. In *The Collected Works* 5, 2nd ed., Bollingen Series XX (Princeton, NJ: Princeton University Press, 1967), p. 29.

36. C. G. Jung, *The Archetypes and the Collective Unconscious*, trans. by R. F. C. Hull. In *The Collected Works* 9, 2nd ed., Bollingen Series XX (Princeton, NJ: Princeton University Press, 1968).

37. See Note 34, p. 152.

Chapter 3

1. Robert Karen, *Becoming Attached: Unfolding the Mystery of the Infant-Mother Bond and Its Impact on Later Life* (New York: Warner Books, 1994).

2. Carroll E. Izard, "On the Ontogenesis of Emotions and Emotion-Cognition Relationships in Infancy." In *The Development of Affect*, ed. by M. Lewis and L. A. Rosenblum (New York: Plenum Press, 1978).

3. T. M. Field et al., "Discrimination and Imitation of Facial Expression by Neonates," *Science* 218 (1982): 179–181.

4. Andrew N. Meltzoff and Richard W. Borton, "Intermodal Matching by Human Neonates," *Nature* 282 (1979): 403–404.

5. René A. Spitz, *The First Year of Life: A Psychoanalytic Study of Normal and Deviant Development of Object Relations* (New York: International Universities Press, 1965).

6. John Bowlby, *Attachment and Loss,* vol. I (New York: Basic Books, 1969).

7. John Bowlby, *Maternal Care and Mental Health.* WHO Monograph Series, no. 2 (Geneva, Switzerland: World Health Organization, 1951).

8. M. D. S. Ainsworth, *Infancy in Uganda: Infant Care and Growth of Love* (Baltimore, MD: The Johns Hopkins University Press, 1967).

9. D. J. Stayton, M. D. S. Ainsworth, and M. B. Main, "Development of Separation Behavior in the First Year of Life: Protest, Following, and Greeting," *Developmental Psychology* 9, no. 2 (1973): 213–225.

10. Mary D. Salter Ainsworth et al., *Patterns of Attachment: A Psychological Study of the Strange Situation* (Hillsdale, NJ: Lawrence Erlbaum, 1978).

11. See Note 1, ch. 12.

12. L. A. Sroufe, "Infant-Caregiver Attachment and Patterns of Adaptation in Preschool: The Roots of Maladaptation and Competence." In *Minnesota Symposium in Child Psychology* 16, ed. by M. Perlmutter (Hillsdale, NJ: Lawrence Erlbaum, 1983), pp. 41–81.

13. See Note 1, p. 202.

14. Harry F. Harlow and Robert P. Zimmerman, "Affectional Responses in the Infant Monkey," *Science* 130 (1959): 421–432.

15. Harry F. Harlow, "The Heterosexual Affectional System in Monkeys," *American Psychologist* 17 (1962): 1–9.

16. Sharon Begley, "How to Build a Baby's Brain," *Newsweek* (Spring/ Summer 1997): 28–32.

17. Allan N. Schore, *Affect Regulation and the Origin of the Self: The Neurobiology of Emotional Development* (Hillsdale, NJ: Lawrence Erlbaum, 1994).

18. J. B. Watson and R. R. Watson, *Psychological Care of Infant and Child,* reprint ed. (New York: Arno Press, 1972) pp. 81–82.

19. Ibid., p. 87.

20. D. W. Winnicott, *Babies and Their Mothers,* ed. by C. Winnicott, R.

Shepherd, and M. Davis (New York: Addison-Wesley, 1987).

21. Phyllis Greenacre, *Trauma, Growth and Personality* (New York: W. W. Norton, 1952), pp. 27–53.

22. Jeffrey Pickens and Tiffany Field, "Facial Expressivity in Infants of Depressed Mothers," *Developmental Psychology* 29, no. 6 (1993): 986–988.

23. Tiffany Field et al., "Relative Right Frontal EEG Activation in 3- to 6-Month-Old Infants of 'Depressed' Mothers," *Developmental Psychology* 31, no. 3 (1995): 358–363.

24. Daniel N. Stern, *The Interpersonal World of the Infant: A View from Psychoanalysis and Developmental Psychology* (New York: Basic Books, 1985).

25. Ibid., p. 140.

26. Margaret S. Mahler, Fred Pine, and Anni Bergman, *The Psychological Birth of the Human Infant: Symbiosis and Individuation* (New York: Basic Books, 1975).

27. See Note 17, ch. 18.

28. Jerome Kagan, *Galen's Prophecy: Temperament in Human Nature* (New York: Basic Books, 1994).

29. D. W. Winnicott, *The Maturational Processes and the Facilitating Environment* (New York: International Universities Press, 1965).

30. Alice Miller, *The Drama of the Gifted Child* (New York: Basic Books, 1981), p. 32.

31. Alice Miller, *Banished Knowledge: Facing Childhood Injuries* (New York: Doubleday, 1990), p. 30.

32. James F. Masterson, *The Search for the Real Self: Unmasking the Personality Disorders of Our Age* (New York: The Free Press, 1988).

33. Heinz Kohut, "Thoughts on Narcissism and Narcissistic Rage," *The Psychoanalytic Study of the Child* 27 (1973): 360–400.

34. See Note 20, p. 90.

35. See Note 17, ch. 25.

36. Harville Hendrix, *Keeping the Love You Find: A Personal Guide* (New York: Pocket Books, 1992), p. 257.

37. Jamie Sams and David Carson, *Medicine Cards: The Discovery of Power through the Ways of Animals* (Santa Fe, NM: Bear and Co., 1988), p. 13.

38. Ibid., pp. 125–126.

39. Core shamanism, as taught by The Foundation for Shamanic Studies, focuses on the direct teachings of the power animals and does not include

interpretations of their essence. The interpretation provided here was adopted from Native American teachings.

40. Kenneth Meadows, *The Medicine Way: A Shamanic Path to Self Mastery* (Rockport, MA: Element, 1990).

41. See Note 37, pp. 113–114.

42. Eugene T. Gendlin, *Focusing*, 2nd ed. (New York: Bantam, 1981).

Chapter 4

1. Charles Darwin, *The Expression of the Emotions in Man and Animals* (1872). Reprinted by the University of Chicago Press, 1965.

2. Konrad Lorenz, *On Aggression* (New York: Bantam Books, 1971).

3. *The Standard Edition of the Complete Psychological Works of Sigmund Freud*, vols. XVIII & XIX, trans. by James Strachey (London, England: The Hogarth Press, 1920, 1923).

4. *Man and Aggression*, ed., by M. F. Ashley Montagu (New York: Oxford University Press, 1968), p. 15.

5. Ashley Montagu, *The Nature of Human Aggression* (New York: Oxford University Press, 1976), p. 21.

6. Sharon Begley, "Grey Matters," *Newsweek* (27 March 1995): 48–54.

7. Jerome Kagan, *Galen's Prophecy: Temperament in Human Nature* (New York: Basic Books, 1994).

8. Ibid., p. 296.

9. Carol Tavris, *Anger: The Misunderstood Emotion*, rev. ed. (New York: Simon & Schuster, 1989), p. 35.

10. Victor LaCerva, *Pathways to Peace: Forty Steps to a Less Violent America* (Tesuque, NM: Heartsong Publications, 1996).

11. See Note 5, ch. 1, p. 11.

12. Michael J. Mahoney, *Human Change Processes: The Scientific Foundations of Psychotherapy* (New York: Basic Books, 1991), p. 157.

13. D. Doumas, G. Margolin, and R. S. John, "The Intergenerational Transmission of Aggression across Three Generations," *Journal of Family Violence* 9, no. 2 (1994): 157–175.

14. Dante Cicchetti and Sheree L. Toth, "A Developmental Psychopathology Perspective on Child Abuse and Neglect," *Journal of the American Academy of Child and Adolescent Psychiatry* 34, no. 5 (1995): 549.

15. René Spitz, *The First Year of Life: A Psychoanalytic Study of Normal and Deviant Development of Object Relations* (New York: International

Universities Press, 1965), p. 106.

16. Heinz Hartmann, Ernest Kris, and Rudolph Loewenstein, "Notes on the Theory of Aggression," *The Psychoanalytic Study of the Child* III/IV (1949): 9–36.

17. Alicia F. Lieberman, *The Emotional Life of the Toddler* (New York: Free Press, 1993), p. 39.

18. Linda C. Mayes and Donald J. Cohen, "The Social Matrix of Aggression: Enactments and Representations of Loving and Hating in the First Years of Life," *The Psychoanalytic Study of the Child* 48 (1993): 145–169.

19. Beata Rank, "Aggression," *The Psychoanalytic Study of the Child* III/IV (1949): 48.

20. Bruno Bettelheim addressed the aggression as well as the oral greediness and pubertal sexual desires implicated in this fairy tale. See Bruno Bettelheim, *The Uses of Enchantment: The Meaning and Importance of Fairy Tales* (New York: Alfred A. Knopf, 1977).

21. Carl Sagan and Ann Druyan, *Shadows of Forgotten Ancestors* (New York: Random House, 1992), pp. 405–406.

22. Z. Y. Kuo, "The Genesis of the Cat's Response to the Rat," *The Journal of Comparative Psychology* XI (1930): 1–35. Cited by Sagan and Druyan (See Note 21).

23. See Note 21, p. 106.

24. Erich Fromm, *The Anatomy of Human Destructiveness* (Greenwich, CT: Fawcett Publications, 1973), p. 303.

25. See Note, 12, p. 199.

Chapter 5

1. Cited in *Psychoanalytic Terms and Concepts*, ed. by Burness E. Moore and Bernard D. Fine (New Haven, CT: The American Psychoanalytic Association and Yale University Press, 1990), p. 32.

2. *The Random House Dictionary of the English Language*, 2nd ed., s.v. "emotion."

3. F. Sherwood Taylor, *The Alchemists* (New York: Arno Press, 1974), p. 3.

4. John Lash, *The Seeker's Handbook* (New York: Crown, 1990), pp. 96–98.

5. See Note 3, p. 236.

6. Mircea Eliade, *Shamanism: Archaic Techniques of Ecstasy*, trans. by W. R. Trask, Bollingen Series LXXVI (Princeton, NJ: Princeton University

Press, 1968), pp. 270–271.

7. C. G. Jung, *Psychology and Alchemy*, trans. by R. F. C. Hull. In *The Collected Works* 12, 2nd ed., Bollingen Series XX (Princeton, NJ: Princeton University Press, 1968), p. 25.

8. C. G. Jung, *The Archetypes and the Collective Unconscious*, trans. by R. F. C. Hull. In *The Collected Works* 9, pt. 1, 2nd ed., Bollingen Series XX (Princeton, NJ: Princeton University Press, 1968), p. 179.

9. Ibid., p. 168.

10. Ibid.

11. Anthony Stevens, *Archetypes: A Natural History of the Self* (New York: Quill, 1983), p. 29.

12. See Note 8, p. 81.

13. C. G. Jung, *Civilization in Transition*, trans. by R. F. C. Hull. In *The Collected Works* 10, 2nd ed., Bollingen Series XX (Princeton, NJ: Princeton University Press, 1970), p. 31.

14. C. G. Jung, *The Symbolic Life*, trans. by R. F. C. Hull. In *The Collected Works* 18, 2nd ed., Bollingen Series XX (Princeton, NJ: Princeton University Press, 1980), p. 253.

15. Ibid., p. 255.

16. Ibid., p. 262.

17. Ibid., p. 254.

18. See Note 13, pp. 82–83.

19. *Meeting the Shadow: The Hidden Power of the Dark Side of Human Nature*, ed. by Connie Zweig and Jeremiah Abrams (Los Angeles: Jeremy P. Tarcher, 1991), p. xxiv.

20. See Note 14.

21. C. G. Jung, *Memories, Dreams, Reflections*, recorded and ed. by Aniela Jaffé, trans. by Richard and Clara Winston (New York: Pantheon, 1961), p. 183.

22. Ibid., p. 184.

23. Anthony Storr, *The Essential Jung* (Princeton, NJ: Princeton University Press, 1983).

Chapter 6

1. George E. Vaillant, *The Wisdom of the Ego* (Cambridge, MA: Harvard University Press, 1993), p. 4.

2. Phyllis Tyson and Robert L. Tyson, *Psychoanalytic Theories of Development: An Integration* (New Haven, CT: Yale University Press, 1990).

3. Vaillant outlines four styles of defense ranging from psychotic to mature. *Psychotic* styles include delusional projection, psychotic denial, and distortion. *Immature* styles are projection, fantasy, hypochondriasis, passive aggression, acting out, and dissociation (neurotic denial). *Neurotic,* or *intermediate,* styles include displacement, isolation of affect (intellectualization), repression, and reaction formation. *Mature* styles of defense include altruism, sublimation, suppression, anticipation, and humor. (See Note 1, ch. 2.)

4. See Note 1, ch. 5.

5. Ibid., p. 8.

6. Ibid., p. 333.

7. Ibid., p. 337.

8. Ibid., p. 340.

9. Michael J. Mahoney, *Human Change Processes: The Scientific Foundations of Psychotherapy* (New York: Basic Books, 1991), pp. 259–260.

10. Ibid., ch. 8.

11. Franz Alexander, *Fundamentals of Psychoanalysis* (New York: W. W. Norton, 1948), p. 28.

12. Leslie S. Greenberg and Jeremy D. Safran, "Emotion in Psychotherapy," *American Psychologist* 44 (1989): 19–29.

13. See Note 9, pp. 263–265.

14. Barry L. Duncan, Mark A. Hubble, and Scott D. Miller, "Stepping Off the Throne," *The Family Therapy Networker* (July/August 1997): 22–33.

15. See Note 9, p. 351.

16. *Meeting the Shadow: The Hidden Power of the Dark Side of Human Nature,* ed. by Connie Zweig and Jeremiah Abrams (Los Angeles: Jeremy P. Tarcher, 1991), pp. xxiv–xxv.

17. Robert Bly, "Eating the Shadow." In *Meeting the Shadow: The Hidden Power of the Dark Side of Human Nature,* ed. by Connie Zweig and Jeremiah Abrams (Los Angeles: Jeremy P. Tarcher, 1991), p. 280.

18. C. G. Jung, *Psychology and Alchemy,* trans. by R. F. C. Hull. In *The Collected Works* 12, 2nd ed., Bollingen Series XX (Princeton, NJ: Princeton University Press, 1968), p. 159.

19. Jolande Jacobi, *The Way of Individuation,* trans. by R. F. C. Hull (New York: New American Library, 1967), p. 130.

20. Ibid., pp. 130–131.

21. Teilhard de Chardin, *Building the Earth* (New York: Avon, 1969), p. 97.

Selected Bibliography

Achterberg, Jeanne. *Imagery in Healing: Shamanism and Modern Medicine.* Boston: Shambhala, 1985.

de Chardin, Teilhard. *Building the Earth.* New York: Avon, 1969.

Eliade, Mircea. *Shamanism: Archaic Techniques of Ecstasy,* trans. by W. R. Trask. Bollingen Series LXXVI. Princeton, NJ: Princeton University Press, 1964.

Harner, Michael. *The Way of the Shaman: A Guide to Power and Healing.* San Francisco: Harper & Row, 1980.

Hergenhahn, B. R. *An Introduction to the History of Psychology,* 2nd ed. Belmont, CA: Wadsworth, 1992.

Ingerman, Sandra. *Soul Retrieval: Mending the Fragmented Self.* San Francisco: Harper, 1991.

Jolande Jacobi, *The Way of Individuation,* trans. by R. F. C. Hall. New York: New American Library, 1967.

Jung, C. G. *The Archetypes and the Collective Unconscious,* trans. by R. F. C. Hull. In *The Collected Works* 9, pt. 1, 2nd ed. Bollingen Series XX. Princeton, NJ: Princeton University Press 1968.

Jung, C. G. *Psychology and Alchemy,* trans. by R. F. C. Hull. In *The Collected Works* 12, 2nd ed. Bollingen Series XX. Princeton, NJ: Princeton University Press, 1968.

Jung, C. G. *The Symbolic Life,* trans. by R. F. C. Hull. In *The Collected Works* 18, 2nd ed. Bollingen Series XX. Princeton, NJ: Princeton University Press, 1980.

Karen, Robert. *Becoming Attached: Unfolding the Mystery of the Infant-Mother Bond and Its Impact on Later Life.* New York: Warner Books, 1994.

Lieberman, Alicia F. *The Emotional Life of the Toddler.* New York: Free Press, 1993.

Mahler, Margaret S., Fred Pine, and Anni Bergman. *The Psychological Birth of the Human Infant.* New York: Basic Books, 1975.

Mahoney, Michael J. *Human Change Processes: The Scientific Foundations of Psychotherapy.* New York: Basic Books, 1991.

Masterson, James F. *The Search for the Real Self: Unmasking the Personality Disorders of Our Age.* New York: The Free Press, 1988.

Mayes, Linda C., and Donald J. Cohen. "The Social Matrix of Aggression: Enactments and Representations of Loving and Hating in the First Years of Life." *The Psychoanalytic Study of the Child* 48 (1993): 145–169.

Miller, Alice. *The Drama of the Gifted Child.* New York: Basic Books, 1981.

Schore, Allan N. *Affect Regulation and the Origin of the Self: The Neurobiology of Emotional Development.* Lawrence Erlbaum: Hillsdale, NJ: 1994.

Simonton, O. Carl, Stephanie Matthews-Simonton, and James Creighton. *Getting Well Again.* Los Angeles: Tarcher, 1978.

Stern, Daniel N. *The Interpersonal World of the Infant: A View from Psychoanalysis and Developmental Psychology.* New York: Basic Books, 1985.

Vaillant, George E. *The Wisdom of the Ego.* Cambridge, MA: Harvard University Press, 1993.

Walsh, Roger N. *The Spirit of Shamanism.* New York: G. P. Putnam, 1990.

Winnicott, D. W. *Babies and Their Mothers,* ed. by C. Winnicott, R. Shepherd, and M. Davis. New York: Addison-Wesley, 1987.

Zweig, Connie, and Jeremiah Abrams, eds. *Meeting the Shadow: The Hidden Power of the Dark Side of Human Nature.* Los Angeles: Jeremy P. Tarcher, 1991.

Index

About the Author

Jeannette M. Gagan, PhD, is a licensed psychologist and a student of shamanism. She links the two disciplines into Shamanic Psychother-apeutics, an approach she teaches to therapists and applies in her clinical practice with adult and adolescent clients. The author of sev-eral published articles on the clinical applications of imagery and the nature and assessment of empathy, she lives in northern New Mexico and is the mother of five children.

Order Form

Quantity		Amount
_____	*Journeying: Where Shamanism and Psychology Meet* ($16.00)	_____
	Sales tax of 6.25% (for New Mexico residents)	_____
	Shipping and handling (see chart below)	_____
	Total amount enclosed	_____

Quantity discounts available

Shipping and Handling

	Surface	First Class	
United States	$2.70	$4.00	plus $1.00 per book on
Canada	$3.20	$4.20	orders of two or more

Method of payment

❑ Check or money order enclosed (made payable to **Rio Chama Publications**, in US currency only)

❑ MasterCard
❑ VISA

Signature _____   Expiration date

Please photocopy this order form, fill it out, and mail it, together with your name, address, and personal check, money order, or charge-card information, to:

RIO CHAMA PUBLICATIONS
PO Box 4276
Santa Fe, NM 87502
800-672-9874